Pink Leadership

15 Life Lessons for ♀ Leaders

all things I seek are
now seeking me.

Pink Leadership

15 Life Lessons for ♀ Leaders

Jeanne Gulbranson

Table of Contents

Acknowledgements   **VII**

Introduction: Why I Wrote This for You   **1**

What Are Your Life Lessons?   4

Chapter 1: What Do You Want to Be?   **5**

Life Lesson #1: On the Path to Success—Maybe   19

Life Lesson #2: The Great Dog Fight   26

Chapter 2: Throw Away the Fool's Gold   **33**

Life Lesson #3: Violins and the Brass...and a Few Renegade Oboes   34

Chapter 3: Don't Be Surprised by the Noise   **57**

Life Lesson #4: Bread, Butter, and Jelly People   57

Chapter 4: Don't Believe the Lies   **63**

Life Lesson #5: Too Many Choices!   67

Life Lesson #6: The Manners Maven   71

Chapter 5: Don't Get Buried   **81**

Life Lesson #7: Shake It Off!   93

Chapter 6: Do What Leaders Do!   101
Life Lesson #8: Just Like His Mother   103

Chapter 7: Nothing Happens Until You Sell Something   113
Life Lesson #9: Step Right Up!   114

Chapter 8: Can You Handle the Truth?   125
Life Lesson #10: Coming Up Roses!   132

Chapter 9: Do the Little Things...Big Things Follow!   141
Life Lesson #11: Veni, Vidi, Vici: Not!   143

Chapter 10: Get What You Want...or Change What You Want   161
Life Lesson #12: Did I Hear You Right?   165

Chapter 11: Walk Tall!   185
Life Lesson #13: Keep Your Pants On!   191
Life Lesson #14: The Mouse That Roared   202

Chapter 12: Just Do It!   207
Life Lesson #15: Powder Puff Mechanics   210

Chapter 13: Who Is the Fairest of Them All?   225
"...And a Child Shall Lead Us"   226

Appendix   231
The Best Blueberry Muffins   231
Peach Cobbler   232
Sophia Loren's Pasta Carbonara   234
Beer Bread   235
Homemade Chocolate Pudding   235

Acknowledgements

THERE ARE SO many powerful, talented...and interesting women and men who helped me write *Pink Leadership*. Many of them just didn't know it at the time! They did let me watch, listen, and learn while they provided the examples, anecdotes, and Life Lessons, however. I regret that I can't remember the names of some of the people who taught me, but many of my stories go way back—past the limitations of my name-memory. I may have forgotten their names, but I definitely remember what they gave me—the opportunity to be a part of their lives, so that I could share them with you.

When I do remember names, I believe in giving credit where it's due. There are some special women and men who you will meet in *Pink Leadership*, as well as others who I appreciate for their contributions to *Pink Leadership*, and to me.

I'm grateful for:

My husband Bill, whose daily demonstrations of love and kindness for everyone in his life have taught me how to be a better person. *I cannot find words eloquent or powerful enough to express how grateful I am that you are in my life.*

The many members of my family who you will meet in *Pink Leadership*. (I remember all of *their* names.) You'll read about the incredible joy and lessons that I've received from my daughter, Julie Alicea, and delightful granddaughter, Carissa. Brother and sister-in-law Jim and Toni Erpenbach and my sisters, Pattie Erpenbach, Geri Patregnani, Carol Pierce, all play a big part in my life and my book. My grandfather, Tony Pecchia, was the much-loved patriarch of our family and was unselfish in sharing his wisdom and love with his family and everyone he met. My niece, Tami Langsdorf, makes me smile whenever I'm around her. *Thank you all for being my well-loved family!*

My colleagues, Darryl La Face and Bob Dickey, with whom I've had multiple working and friendship relationships. I've worked for each of them, they have both worked for me, and we've worked together as peers—and I've enjoyed all of it. *Thank you both for the many years of being able to listen, watch, laugh with, and learn from both of you!*

Lemma Gailani, who has allowed me to help her achieve what she was always meant to be—an incredible woman and a superior leader. *Thank you for letting me support you!*

Dr. Michael Crovetti, whose regard for his patients' comfort matches his considerable skills in medicine and business. *Thank you for caring about your patients as people—and thanks also for my great knee!*

Paul Robson, who continues to earn my respect for being the quality person and leader that he is. *Thank you for all the support and great life lessons you've given me, and for lots of laughing together!*

My wonderful dog Patches (who never has a bad day), my Latin teacher, the produce guy at Von's Supermarket, and the warehouse supervisor who cried in Madrid.

Jessica Loving, my editor, who never hesitated to ask, *"What were you thinking when you wrote that?"* when my thoughts sprouted wings and flew away. (Besides offering great editorial advice, she also knows when to use "that" or "which," which I believe elevates her skill level to an unattainable and mysterious height!)

Introduction:
Why I Wrote This for You

I'VE ALWAYS BEEN a real fan of women, and not just because I happen to be one. There's just so much to admire and respect about women—and the incredibly diverse talents that women possess are high on the list. There simply isn't anything that women cannot do—when we feel like it. (Being capricious, and getting away with it, is one of the female traits that I particularly admire.) Women can swap roles in a heartbeat to play whatever part they need to. When the rest of the world needs a partner, a warrior, a wife, a leader, a mother, a team player, a negotiator, a student, a handyman, a lover, an artist, a teacher, a caretaker—the **same** woman can fill all these roles. And she can do it all in the same day. Because of the diversity of roles that we assume by choice or by need, we have tremendous (and fearsome) power over just about anything and anyone—when we choose to exercise it. What's not to admire about women?

I also like things that are uncomplicated and straightforward. There is lots of "chatter" about how complicated women are. That's just a smokescreen that we throw up to prevent the other gender from knowing all our secrets. The truth is that, basically, we are not that complex. We know that we want respect, attention, and all the good things that we deserve. That's pretty simple. (There is some complexity and ambiguity in knowing **exactly** how to deliver on the "respect, attention, and all the good things." Oh well...that uncertainty is part of why women are also so interesting. Besides, there is also adventure and enjoyment in discovering what is included in "all the good things.") We want to be able to do and *"Be All that (We) Can Be"* without joining the Army, unless we also want to do that. (If you are thinking that all the good things I've said about women do not apply to every woman, I agree with you. There are always exceptions. But those exceptions would probably not be reading this book anyway.)

Let's set the expectations appropriately, right from the beginning. *Pink Leadership* is **not** a book that:

▶ Bashes men. I don't hate men—I don't even dislike most of them. In fact, there are lots of men that I respect and admire. You'll be meeting some of them in this book.

▶ Claims that women are better than men. Women are different from men—but not necessarily better, or worse. (Although there are a few things that most women are decidedly better at than most men—but we won't get too hung up on the details.) Overall, I don't believe that women are better. We're just different.

▶ Provides excuses about why women haven't achieved or been able to do...whatever. I offer some reasons for our unique challenges, but *Pink Leadership* is in the no-whine zone.

Pink Leadership is for all the talented, powerful...and interesting women who want the respect and attention they deserve, and for those who are willing to go after and work for "all the good things." *Pink Leadership* is about being all that you can be. If you choose to be a superior leader, either in business and/or in your community, then that's what you should be able to do.

One of the special characteristics of women is that we prefer to know how to do something before we jump right into the fray. (Most of us do read the directions that come with everything.) Another excellent female trait is that we like to learn. We not only enjoy the knowledge, we also enjoy the process. We go to classes, and read self-help books, and explore our ideas with others. We visit museums, watch the Discovery Channel, and go to book clubs and study groups. We watch others, we listen carefully...and we remember. (If there's a woman who can't quote an important (or just about any) conversation **word-for-word**, then I haven't met her yet. Besides the verbatim recall, most women can mimic the facial expressions of every person in the conversation, provide details on what they were wearing, and describe how the place was decorated. They can do all this while simultaneously cooking dinner, driving, putting on makeup, or changing a baby's diaper. Now, **that** is inspired, special talent!) We remember what we've seen and heard, and we learn—that's where the power of women comes from.

We all learn from our own experiences with other women, men, children, colleagues, animals, friends, and enemies. *Pink Leadership* brings the leadership lessons that I've seen and heard and remember from simply living and watching, listening and remembering. The Life Lessons I offer are straightforward and uncomplicated—the way good learning should be. *Pink Leadership* offers **my** lessons from life.

What Are Your Life Lessons?

You likely have many **Life Lessons** that have served you well as you've developed personally and professionally. I'm sure your mother taught you to share—it's time to put her lesson to use.

Go to my Web site (**www.jeannegulbranson.com**) to share your lessons.

Each **Life Lesson** submitted will receive a personal response from me, and many of your lessons will be showcased on the Web site.

Share your bounty! We learn best by teaching others!

CHAPTER 1
What Do You Want to Be?

WHY DON'T WOMEN rule the world? At the least, why don't we hold most of the top spots in all companies? Have we stopped ourselves from achieving our rightful positions of leadership and power, or have "they"? Why is it newsworthy when a woman is the first mayor, police chief, or governor of...some place? A woman runs for president and another woman is a vice-presidential nominee and these are "ground-breaking" events? That's just not right. These events shouldn't be ground-breaking—they should be normal and natural, "how it's supposed to be." But they're not. What—are we amazed that the lizard can talk? Who believes that a female world leader or corporate executive or political powerhouse is an anomaly? Does anyone out there think that women leaders are not "real" women—that they are not acting the way they are "supposed to"? If you believe this, identify yourself so that I can smack some sense into you.

How is it possible that leadership ability is gender-specific? Can it be that some people still believe any or all of the following assumptions?

> ► **The possession of a penis or a uterus grants or excludes leadership ability.**

Do any anatomy books call out the "leadership spot" in genitalia in either sex? I know about the G-Spot[1], but I've never heard of an "L-Spot."

▶ **Men are smarter than women.**
Don't even go there! If this is true, just when would "smarter" have appeared in one sex or the other? When there was just a fertilized egg? Is it possible that "more intelligence" is carried on the Y chromosome? Not likely—or we would certainly have heard about that.

▶ **Men have more time to assume leadership positions while women are time-constrained by having children and raising families.**
This assumption has some truth to it. Women do have more to do. They do bear children and still have (even in our enlightened "role-equality" era) more direct family responsibilities. Does this mean that men should be the leaders because they have more "bench time"? Because men don't (or can't) do as many different things as women, does that make them the best leadership candidates, or just the "available" ones? It sounds like the song, *"If you can't be with the one you love, love the one you're with."* Is it possible that the rest of us are settling for less than the best leadership because we can't all work together to get through some interesting logistics of how to successfully combine disparate roles? What kind of sense does that make?

Or is the challenge the fact that many women interrupt their education and/or careers to take time to raise families? This is another truth. And of course, when the women

---

[1] If you don't know what a G-Spot is—I'm not telling you. You need to look this up.

return to the work force, they get little or no credit for the on-the-job learning and application of all the skills they had to perfect and acquire while they were "just" raising kids. The fact that they have spent (possibly several) years as negotiators, delegators, strategists, planners, accounting managers, and in a plethora of other roles at home just doesn't seem to count. No credit—it's the bottom rung of the ladder for the returning-to-work women. That's just not right either.

▶ **Women don't want to be leaders.**
This statement is seriously misinformed prejudice—an excuse born from bias. It's from the same keep-women-in-their-place attitude as, *"Women don't want to vote, drive, own property, or serve in the military."* Women have proven that these other prejudices are wrong. Women don't want to be leaders? That is craziness.

▶ **People don't want to follow a female leader.**
There appears to be some truth to this one too. According to a 2008 article in the McClatchy newspapers: "Men and women agree that women are more honest, intelligent, compassionate, outgoing and creative, according to a survey out Monday. But men still get a significant edge as leaders—and from both sexes. In a 2008 survey by the Pew Research Center, 69 percent of the over 2,000 people surveyed thought that men and women made equally strong leaders. But only 6 percent said women made better leaders while 21 percent said men did. Men and women held those views almost equally. 'You've got a public that on some level has a complex mix of views on this subject: admiring of women, admiring of traits that they associate with leadership, (but) not yet admiring of women in top leadership roles,' said Paul Taylor,

the lead author of the report and the executive vice president at the research center. He said the researchers hadn't 'cracked the code' for the contradictory findings."

It's not so hard to crack that code. It's difficult for all of us—both women and men—to overcome 200+ years of American history and bias! When we don't really know what to expect, we shy away from it. We don't really know what to expect if the majority of our leadership is female— it's never happened. So, we naturally hold on to what we have now—whether it's wonderful or not. *"It may be a three-legged, diseased dog, but it's **my** dog!"*

► **Men have the inherent characteristics required for leadership and women do not.**
To test this assumption, let's look at the definition of leadership and determine how or if it applies to only men or only women. This is easier said than done.

Trying to Define Leadership

First of all, there are too many definitions of "leadership." Google "definition leadership" and you'll find more than 726,000 entries! I have many awards, plaques, commendations, cards, and e-mails from supervisors, colleagues, and employees commending me for "superior leadership." For most of my life, however, I've had difficulty recognizing **exactly** what I did to merit this praise. I have never (thankfully!) experienced a Rudy Giuliani 9/11 moment, when his powerful and obvious leadership was eloquently displayed. I've never had Oprah Winfrey opportunities to publicly influence millions of people to be and live better by the sheer force of my personal integrity (and the benefits of multi-media coverage). I've never really recognized myself doing "leadership things." I don't ever remember saying, *"Wow, Jeanne—what* *you just did was really great leadership!"* In a Blanche Dubois kind of way, *"I have always depended on the kindness of strangers,"* to affirm that I've provided the leadership they wanted and needed.

I don't believe that I'm unusual in not being able to recognize in myself the actions that define "great leadership." You may have the same challenge. I've sometimes relied on the leadership definition *du jour* (the one that appealed to me the day I needed it) to explain or teach the elusive concepts of influence, motivation, integrity, trust, and all the other skills that attempt to define leadership. For too many lists of leadership skills, try googling the words "list leadership skills"— about 665,000 entries! We need to pare down those leadership definitions and lists to something that we can actually work with.

In my 20+ years of teaching leadership skills, I've finally come to accept this definition and this list of characteristics: *Leaders are passionate, respected, and brave individuals who supply and apply a balanced, change-ready strategy to fulfill their needs and dreams, and the needs and dreams of others.*

My working list of leadership traits includes the following characteristics:

▶ Enthusiasm and passion
▶ Trustworthiness and honesty
▶ Authenticity and respectfulness in their approach to others
▶ Comfort and calm with change or ambiguity
▶ Confidence
▶ Bravery

Now, just which characteristics are exclusively male or female? None of them! It just isn't true that any kind of leadership is gender-specific. Nor is "good" leadership gender-specific. Men (any or all men) are not better leaders than women, nor are women (any or all women) better leaders than men. There are certainly good and bad leaders of both genders. Sex alone does not mean that a person should or can lead well. Regardless of gender, the leader-candidates need to be raised, trained, educated, coached, mentored, and provided with the opportunity to be good leaders.

Another thing that is not true—women (or men) don't **have** to choose to be leaders. They can also choose to be successful, quality followers. (See my book, *Be the Horse or the Jockey*, which explores the role and how-to of professional followership.) The important factor is the ability to choose. A quality individual—either male or female— who possesses the foundational intelligence and innate skills that can be developed into true leadership ability has the right to make the choice to be a leader and to act on it. That's the bottom line—that's how it should be.

So Where Are All the Women Leaders?

Why aren't there more women in leadership positions? There are likely many reasons why executive offices aren't filled with women. Some of the significant reasons include the following:

> ► **Some women buy into some or all of the false assump-tions that I previously listed.**
>   At some level, too many women still believe that men are the first (or only) right choice for leaders. Some women view themselves as not smart enough, not strong enough, or not... something enough to make the choice to be a leader. This view is wrong because the assumptions are not valid. But the feeling of unworthiness persists and holds some women back. They don't "go for it." Part of the hesitation is related to the next two reasons why there aren't more women in leadership positions: history and being seduced.

How do you get past this? Don't believe the false assumptions! Review the reasons why the assumptions don't make sense and refuse to listen to anyone (or yourself) who tries to sell you on that craziness. Just ignore what is not true!

▶ **The history of women's rights (which by association includes the right to lead) has moved very slowly.**
Consider some of these events in the evolution of women as "worthy" individuals—and do the math on how long it took to get from one milestone to another.

- 1848: The first women's rights convention is held in Seneca Falls, New York. After two days of discussion and debate, 68 women and 32 men sign a Declaration of Sentiments, which outlines grievances and sets the agenda for the women's rights movement. A set of 12 resolutions is adopted calling for equal treatment of women and men under the law and voting rights for women.

- 1869: Susan B. Anthony and Elizabeth Cady Stanton form the National Woman Suffrage Association. The primary goal of the organization is to achieve voting rights for women by means of a Congressional amendment to the Constitution.
  (Not too bad...this was only 21 years later.)

- 1920: The 19th Amendment to the Constitution, granting women the right to vote, is signed into law. (Not too great—that took 72 years from the time of the first resolution to grant voting rights.)

- 1961: President John Kennedy establishes the President's Commission on the Status of Women and appoints Eleanor Roosevelt as chairwoman. The report issued by the Commission in 1963 documents substantial discrimination against women in the workplace and makes specific recommendations for improvement, including fair hiring practices, paid maternity leave, and affordable child care.

- 1963: Congress passes the Equal Pay Act, making it illegal for employers to pay a woman less than what a man would receive for the same job. (This is just wrong *prima facie*. Why did we even need a law for this? Same job, same pay—shouldn't that have been a given? Unless...women just weren't considered as valuable as men to begin with, so that's why they had to be called out specifically and "protected." Hmmm...)

- 1968: The Equal Employment Opportunity Commission (EEOC) rules that sex-segregated help-wanted ads in newspapers are illegal. This ruling is upheld in 1973 by the Supreme Court, opening the way for women to apply for higher-paying jobs previously open only to men. (Nice trick. Just avoid having to pay women the good pay by excluding them from the well-paid jobs. Undoing that injustice took 10 years from the time that Congress beneficently granted women the same pay for the same work. That's not exactly impressive.)

- 1972: The Equal Rights Amendment (ERA) is passed by Congress and sent to the states for ratification. Originally drafted by Alice Paul in 1923 (50 years earlier!), the amendment reads: "Equality of rights under the law shall not be denied or abridged by the United

States or by any State on account of sex." The amendment died in 1982 when it failed to achieve ratification by a minimum of 38 states.[2] The proposal has been introduced in every Congress since 1982 but still remains un-ratified. (Legislators believed that women needed to have their inferior status legally fixed, since good common sense and basic human respect wasn't getting the job done. But even the legislature hasn't gotten the job done!)

Since it's been, to date, 160 years since the first 100 men and women got together to start moving women from second-class to equal-class, it's likely going to take a little longer for women and men to accept that women are also worthy, qualified, and eligible to be superior leaders.

How do you get past this? Don't use history as an excuse. You don't want to hide behind, *"It's been like this for 160 years and it's not getting any better any time soon. Why bother trying?"* Shrug off the too slow, lame attempts to rectify an unjust situation. Are **we** the ones who were unable to fix this in 160 years? No. Women have never controlled the legislative bodies that can't get the job done. Sorry for **them**, not for us.

▶ **It's very seductive to be "taken care of."**
Sometimes we are our own worst enemies! It's tempting to retreat into a male-ruled, "witness protection program" when we are tired and overburdened. We want to be hidden away from danger. We want someone else to make

---

[2] The 15 states whose legislatures have not ratified the Equal Rights Amendment are Alabama, Arizona, Arkansas, Florida, Georgia, Illinois, Louisiana, Mississippi, Missouri, Nevada, North Carolina, Oklahoma, South Carolina, Utah, and Virginia.

the hard decisions when we have reached our own limits. We want someone else to fend off the enemies—although usually after we've stirred them up. When our eyes are sleep-deprived red and our minds are full of too much that's too hard, we sometimes want to curl up and be a "furry kitten."

How do you get past this? You don't have to. It's okay to be a furry kitten and to be taken care of for short periods of time and in the privacy of your own home. The problem arises if you bring the purring into the boardroom and want someone to take care of you there too. That is not going to happen, and you've just shot yourself in your own cute little paw (in addition to setting a bad precedent for other women around you who may not want to be treated like furry kittens at work).

► **There's a glass ceiling.**
We all know that it's still there. The last 160 years of looking for equality and the too-long wait for the Equal Rights Amendment notwithstanding, there is still the perception that women are not quite right or ready for many top leadership and management responsibilities. Why is the perception still there? If I knew all the reasons why, I'd tell you and we could shatter that glass ceiling together. I do believe that one of the reasons why the perception and the ceiling are still intact is the insecurity of the men who installed the ceiling and who are currently in charge of keeping it safe and whole. (Although not necessarily clean. Most men I know don't do windows.) Certainly, women have no exclusive claim on being insecure. There is little gender-exclusive possession of feelings of unworthiness. What will happen if women are the leaders? Is it possible that they will be better than the men? When I

think about this possibility from a man's perspective, I can understand why they want the ceiling in place. If I were a man, and I was smart enough to recognize just how good women leaders are, I would probably be concerned about the possibility that "some woman" was going to "show me up." I'd probably try to keep her in her place too! Powerful women are very threatening to the fragile male ego. Oh well...does that mean that we shouldn't be allowed to achieve all that we can—because we might hurt their feelings? No.

The glass ceiling is disguised in many organizations because the word is out—it's not politically correct to hold back women. But it's still there. It is substantially thinner in some organizations that are trying hard to provide the same opportunities across genders, but it's not easy to undo years of the "good ol' boy network." It's still there.

Many years ago, I read about a woman who was attempting to re-enter the business world as a supervisor for a telecommunications company after a multi-year hiatus raising four children. Responding to the question of "Business Experience and Skills," she listed the ability to prioritize, organize, and motivate four children (and a husband) to get up while she made breakfast and got them all dressed and out the door on time with lunch pails and completed homework in hand. She listed skills in coaching (for homework and soccer), planning, team-building, and report-writing (all that homework!), as well as patience and persistence. She included in her explanation how these skills and abilities transferred from her life experiences to the business environment. She did not get the job because she didn't have experience in the telecommunications field. In this case, she did hit gender-induced ignorance. The men who were interviewing her didn't recognize the skills that her experience was bringing to them. She got no credit for what she had learned and practiced in her home life. The glass ceiling she hit was right over the front door of the company to which she applied. I would have hired her, and then taught her about telecommunications. She already had what is extremely difficult to learn or to teach—all the skills in dealing with people, and the ability to apply the knowledge gained to different situations.

In contrast, there is another woman I would **not** have hired! I had a dear friend who was the Director of Admissions for a medical school. She told me about a female applicant who had not scored well on her MCAT (Medical College Admission Test). In an attempt to counter her low score, she wrote a letter to the Admissions Board explaining that her less-than-stellar test results were *"because of the unfortunate timing of my menstrual cycle."* Now, this woman was asking to be allowed to care for the sick and dying and potentially to operate on people. Was she saying she was only capable of quality work three weeks out of every four? That's what the Admissions Board read, and the woman was not accepted into the school. Hers was a case of, "I am Woman...Take Pity on Me."

How do you get past this? Disguised or thin, the glass ceiling holds us back more than it should, just because we know it's there. Yes, the gender-specific limitation is an irritating and unacceptable reality, but it should not frame how we perceive and present ourselves. We certainly don't want to justify our failures (which we will all have!) or hide behind any bias as an excuse. Just know the ceiling is there, but continue to push up against it. Other women have slipped past it and lived well (although sometimes a little bloodied and beaten up). But still, they've gotten past the ceiling and you can too!

Unfortunately, there are some women in business who choose to perceive themselves as "victims." Women are not victims. If we believe that we are, we will act that way, and we will then become victims—of our self-fulfilling prophesy. We should not choose to be victims. Victims are not leaders. Helen Reddy said it right with, "I am Woman, Hear me Roar!"

We are not the same as men; we are not even the same as our sisters, mothers, or best friends. We are who we are, and we are valuable in our own right. We are not victims, and we should never portray ourselves in a pitiful way.

▶ **We choose to place a higher priority on children and family life over the extraordinary time and consistent dedication it takes to get to the top of the corporate ladder.**
Women often consciously decide to interrupt their education and/or careers in order to devote their full time and attention to children and families. In many cases, this creates a negative effect on a woman's ability to achieve the leadership position she would have striven for and for which she is well-qualified.

How do you get past this? You don't have to. You have choices; and the choice of family over career (for a time or for always) is a worthy option. A career choice to take care of children and/or other family members is as honorable and valuable a career choice as any corporate leadership position. (Besides, your local charities, schools, and volunteer organizations also need superior leaders. Your skills never have to go unwanted or stale!)

Assume the Position—The One in Front!

If you have chosen to be a valued leader, how do you take your rightful place at the head of the pack? First of course, you need the knowledge of what a leader is and does, but you also need hard work and a good sense of humor—because it's not going to be easy, and sometimes, you just need to laugh at your own struggle. (Laughing beats crying about it. Cry and you'll stop trying—laugh and you'll plunge forward.)

The good news about acquiring the knowledge we need to lead effectively is that women appear to be on a perpetual quest to learn. I don't know the reasons why—maybe it's curiosity, or mental energy, or the need to build our self-esteem. Or maybe it's survival. For whatever reason, who do you see at most classes at your work that are "optional"? Who do you see at the continuing education courses at your local community college? Who buys and reads the most self-help books? Women. We're so hungry to learn that we don't wait for someone to bring it on—we go after it!

Pink Leadership will bring it on (and let you go after it) with the leadership lessons that come from both our personal and professional lives. Lessons don't have to be difficult to be good. Most of what you'll learn about working and success in the business world has and will come from the simpler things in life.

We hear and say very often in business: *"Keep it simple. Tell me in words that I can understand."* But our actions frequently belie our words. Too often, we listen to the person with the complex charts and tricky pivot tables in thick, three-ring binders. It must be right—look at how complicated it is! (It's even more credible, of course, if there are more than three colors on the charts.) While I'm not casting aside the need (in select situations) for complicated concepts and presentations, the most powerful leaders in business, government, and life know how to make things simple. That's one of the things that women seem to know how to do as well—we know how to make things simple. Why shouldn't we? We've had lots of practice teaching kids why they won't get the Xbox they're whining for and explaining to husbands why the gutters need to be cleaned out now. In this first, simple **Life Lesson** we'll find out how best to learn to travel the path to success.

Life Lesson #1: On the Path to Success—Maybe

I was fifteen years old when I got my first, after-school job as a waitress in my busy, hometown diner. The delight about earning my own money skyrocketed when I got my first tip. Someone just gave me $0.25 *extra* for doing my job! I was headed down the path to professional and financial success! My joy diminished a few days later when I received my first paycheck. At the prevailing waitress pay rate of $5.00 a shift, my check was $20.00. Adding the $27.80 in tips I had earned barely allowed me to start repaying my mother for the cost of the $13.00 white uniform and the $25.00 ugly, waitress shoes I had to buy for the job. My path to professional success had taken a curve. I had some decisions to make—quit this craziness or get a lot better at it.

I decided to become a world-class waitress in a small-town diner. I definitely needed to improve my skills as a waitress. Somehow, those tips had to go way up! I asked the owner of the restaurant for his advice. He responded with, *"Never walk with your hands empty."*

Only after pondering the owner's cryptic statement while working many more long, lunch and dinner shifts did I realize that he had handed me a valuable **Life Lesson.** *"Never walk with your hands empty"* meant that I need to:

- ► *Do more with less effort*
- ► *Learn to prioritize and plan*
- ► Always be picking up new lessons—new learning

I don't know if I ever became a world-class waitress, but I sure made more money when I never walked with my hands empty!

Almost 40 years later, I repeated this story to my colleague, mentor, and friend, Darryl La Face[3]. (Please see the footnote. I believe in giving credit where it's due and will always "call out" those people who deserve applause. However, if a person needs a good slap on the head, they will be referred to as "a person who needs to remain nameless.") His eyes widened in amazement when I came to the "punch line" of not walking with your hands empty. *"That's what my mother taught me when I was very young! She said exactly the same thing! Now, I understand what she was telling me!"* Darryl's mother was an artist who was always seen with a pen and paper in hand. She was always ready to see and capture the next image. Darryl has spent his life alert to Life's Lessons. He just hadn't realized where he had learned that lesson. (How typical is that? A valuable lesson taught by his mother... and he didn't even know it!)

---

[3] Darryl La Face is the Managing Director of ADJ Consulting, a firm that aligns human capital with business performance. Darryl has worked for me, I have worked for him, and we have worked together as peers. Throughout our various relationships, he has provided a good ear, sage counsel, and lots of delightful and often therapeutic laughter.

Never Walk With Your Hands Empty

This is the advice that has guided my entire professional (and personal) life. There are valuable life and business lessons all around us, as long as we never walk with our hands (or heads) empty. I have gathered and repeated anecdotes from the diverse experiences of my varied careers as mother, business owner, corporate strategist, executive coach, professional skills trainer, speaker, school director, and occasional antiques dealer. I've often heard, *"You have all the great stories! So many interesting things have happened to you! Things like that just don't happen to me."* The truth is that interesting, insightful things happen to all of us. They happen to you! It's a matter of never walking with your head empty. Career lessons are all around us. You just have to be ready to listen to, recognize, receive, and grow from them. Never walk with your head empty.

My personal prejudice is that women have more opportunities to receive and benefit from Life's Lessons because we are all about diversity in experiences. Many of us have, or have had, separate but overlapping lives as mothers, wives, schedulers, personal shoppers, cooks, housekeepers, chauffeurs, counselors, jailers—in addition to being business managers, nurses, CEOs, teachers, customer service representatives, and waitresses.

In my personal quest to learn (and then to teach) all I could about leadership, I searched for the Holy Grail of leadership. What is the one most valuable skill to learn and perfect that will make the difference between wanting and trying and actually succeeding? After years of looking and learning and providing "superior leadership" (and wondering just how that happened), I found the Holy Grail. It is **listening**. Listening is the beginning of knowing exactly what you need to do to be a premier leader.

No one person has all the answers to the challenges we face in life and in business, so we have many reasons to listen and many people to listen to. There are, of course, the obvious benefits of listening: gathering significant data and receiving different perspectives to resolve problems. Related to the ability to lead, however, listening is also a demonstration to others that you value their input, are carefully weighing all options, and as a consequence, can be trusted to make the right decisions. One of the simpler definitions among the 726,000 Google choices for leadership is, "Having followers." We all want and need to be listened to. A leader who listens is the person we are apt to believe in and follow. My conclusion, from my own experience and from observing and listening to others, is, *"If we do not listen well, we will not lead well."*

This revelation came to me from Lemma Gailani, a young woman born in Afghanistan and raised in Pakistan and the United States. She is now a U.S. citizen, and she is also a strong, emerging leader. Part of my role as Strategist with CIBER, Inc.[4] is to provide training in strategic, professional skills to the company's consultants. To accomplish this training, I developed a year-long Project Manager Development (PMD) course that focuses not only on the "mechanics" of project management, but on the "art" as well. One of the self-study elements includes reading a specified course book, with exercises, and then completing a written assignment on listening skills. Lemma was a candidate in the PMD program and submitted the most insightful and courageously introspective response to her listening skills assignment that I had ever read.[5] She obviously spent considerable time and thinking on listening. She enlisted others to help her practice and evaluate her skills and progress. Her plan for continuing listening development was well thought-out and realistic. She had recognized an even greater value of the skill of listening than I

---

[4] CIBER, Inc. is an international consulting firm specializing in information systems integration for both private and government sector clients. CIBER has 85+ offices in 18 countries with 8,500 employees.

[5] I wish I could share Lemma's entire response with you, but that would unfairly violate her privacy. Just trust me on this—she definitely understood the lesson of the importance of listening!

had—the opportunity to engage others appropriately and willingly in support of her quest to excel. Lemma's response and the intensity of her focus caused me to re-think the mystery of great leadership. Is it really so indecipherable? No, it is not. With her self-examination and the strong importance she placed on this art, Lemma validated and cemented for me the belief that the key to the best in leadership is listening. I learned as much from her assignment as she did!

The fact that Lemma worked very hard on the assignment and chose to share her own story and her insight is indicative of the values and behaviors that will serve her well in her development as a leader. She is brave, earnest, sincere, authentic, hard-working, and insightful—and she listens very well. If you want to be a leader, or you want to perfect your skills as a leader, then be a Lemma!

One of the reasons that people follow those who listen well is that they often like them. We tend to buy from and buy into people who are like us and who we like. Good listeners are usually just more likeable than talkers! My sister-in-law, Toni Erpenbach,[6] is a superior listener. Her listening skills are actually necessary for her acceptance and survival in an over-talking, Italian family full of sisters who always have something (lots!) to say about everything. Everyone wants to sit by Toni at the dinner table. She listens! And when she does begin to talk, *we* all listen. She must have something good to say—she's been listening to all of us expound on every subject imaginable! People gravitate towards good listeners. One of the requirements of being a leader is to have followers. Listen and they will come.

Listening, with your ears and your eyes, is how you will never walk with your head empty. It is the way you develop into a superior leader.

---

[6] Toni Erpenbach, married to "little" brother Jim, is a retired High School Counselor, horse-woman, certified hypnotist, and grandmother. She also seems to be getting even more beautiful as she gets older. That, to the rest of the women in our family, is not one of her more endearing characteristics.

Complex leadership skill sets, with the willingness and ability to apply them, are unique to each individual. You can admire and attempt to emulate great leaders, but you cannot provide leadership in the exact way they do. You cannot do exactly the same things. You are not the same person. Listen to others and then personalize, practice, and perfect your own skills. Learn to recognize and develop your personal characteristics of leadership—working with others toward a common goal. Never walk with your head empty. Listen—listen over and over and over again.

Now you know. You know:

- ▶ You have the right to choose to be a superior leader (or a professional follower). You do not have to believe those crazy assumptions made by other people.

- ▶ The definition of a leader and the skills they possess are not gender-specific. You have them in at least the same measure (or maybe more) as do Tom and Jim and Fred.

- ▶ Some of the main reasons why more women like you haven't "taken over the world"… and you've begun to see how to get around them.

- ▶ The first Life Lesson: *Never walk with your head empty.*

The Choice is Yours

You have choices, so…what do you want to be when you grow up? How many times have you been asked, or asked yourself, this question? Regardless of your age right now, this could still be an open issue. Did you start out with ballerina, nurse, cowgirl, mother, or teacher? It was so much easier to answer this question when we were younger, wasn't it? We had such definitive goals with occupations and roles that had specific titles! Somewhere around 12 years old, however, the answer to this question became more ambiguous. You may have started to respond with, "*I don't know.*"

Despite the lack of a definite title, at some point during your career choice musings, a subtle desire to be a "leader" may have started to emerge in you. Lily Tomlin said, "*When I was younger, I always wanted to grow up and be somebody. Now I know I should have been more specific.*" You may not have gotten more specific about wanting to be a leader early on, but that's how you began to act and what you began to work toward. That's what you wanted to achieve—a position of leadership in whatever profession or industry you found yourself, where the roles and titles have definite names.

Leadership ability often first appears in the sandbox and on the playground and takes on its own evolutionary life through the school years. But at some point, you will be as good as you will be without a conscious decision, focused attention, and commitment to continue to develop as a leader. We have all experienced "mutant" leaders. These are the potentially great leaders who have morphed into wanna-bes, bullies, tyrants, or legend-in-their-own-mind types. Maybe they would have been real leaders, but they did not choose to devote attention, time, and energy to becoming the best that they could be.

This wanna-be must not be you. You're reading *Pink Leadership*! You must have made (or are making) the decision to be a superior leader in your professional or personal life. Good for you! But, do you know what you're signing up for? Making a fully-informed decision includes being ready for what you ask for. You may not want to buy a pony if you live in an apartment—unless you also own a stable. It's good to know all the implications as you move from a nascent playground leader to a captain of industry. Another **Life Lesson** is coming up.

Life Lesson #2: The Great Dog Fight

All of us who were there will never forget the day of the great dog fight!

Oh, the lure of pastoral, southeast Missouri: bucolic, lush trees and flowers with almost no insects—flying or crawling! A post-card-perfect scene enhanced by a gorgeous winding river below a high bluff cleared for camping. Perfect for resting and playing in the fresh air and sun! Anyway, that's the description that my brother, Jim Erpenbach,[7] used to entice me to join them for a long weekend camping trip. Jim and his wife Toni, along with their two young sons, were camping with their friends, Jim and Linda Cartee, and their young daughter. Although Cartee had a broken leg and was confined to crutches, brother Jim assured me that even Cartee was enjoying it.

I do not go camping! I do not go anywhere that doesn't have a bathroom with a locking door, and I definitely don't sleep on the ground—I have a Princess and the Pea problem. But I agreed to join them for one day only (no night!) of fun and frolic—Ugghhh! My husband and children packed bathing suits and food while I threw in a large amount of patience as my contribution, and we made our way to the river. Jim said we should bring our German Shepherd, Sarge, because Jim's family had their Irish Setter, Mr. Bo Jangles (Bo), and the dogs would really enjoy playing together.

(You can likely feel what's coming, right?)

---

[7] At the time of this story, Jim was the local high school basketball coach and was passionately committed to his family, friends, and teams, and to outdoor recreation. Jim is now a retired high school principal and still lives in the small town where we grew up. He has continued during his retirement to provide superior leadership to his community as the champion (and workhorse) for the community park and an elected school board member. Jim is still passionately committed to his family, friends, and community, and to outdoor recreation.

To appreciate what happened, you need to know how Jim was at the time of the memorable camping trip. Sometime around his tenth birthday, Jim tired of being the skinny little boy that the big kids picked on all the time, and he started lifting weights. In a remarkably short amount of time, Jim became one of the big kids! From junior high school on, he was the strongest, toughest kid we'd ever seen. We all knew, and more importantly Jim knew, that in any fight, he would be the victor! (He proved that more than a few times in high school.) We called him Mongo for his unfortunate tendency to accidentally break almost anything he touched just by his hard-to-control brute strength. (In fact, Mongo was the cause of his friend Cartee's broken leg. When wiry Cartee jumped on Jim's head from the roof of a garage they were painting together earlier that summer, Jim threw Cartee off his head, and...voila...broken leg! In reparation, Jim did all Cartee's yard work and carried him everywhere that summer, including to the camping trip.)

When my family arrived at the campsite, Jim's dog Bo immediately came bounding over with the express purpose of attacking our dog! A brief skirmish ensued, but both Bo and Sarge were leashed, so Jim managed to separate them before anything really ugly happened. Jim decided that we should just tie the dogs to trees far enough apart for safety but where they could see each other so they could start *"getting used to each other."*

A few hours later, Jim decided it was time for the dogs to make friends. *"Yep, I think they're ready now. I'm going to put them together and you just watch—they'll play nice,"* he said definitively. Jim slapped the arm of his lawn chair for emphasis, bending the metal arm as he stood up. We all snickered and rolled our eyes. Jim's wife Toni, who has always had the best sense of all of us, urged him to stop. *"Jim, I wouldn't do that. There's 200 pounds of dog there. They don't like each other. I don't think you should do that!"* Jim could not be dissuaded, however. The dogs were coming together.

Jim walked Bo to within about six feet of Sarge and then unleashed both dogs. Immediately, they jumped at each other with bared teeth and ear-splitting growling with Jim between them! And he stayed between them! The sounds and sights that followed the initial assault were horror-picture quality.

Mixed with the continuous and horrendous sound of two large dogs attacking each other were the loud shouts of, *"Get the kids! Oh my God—stop them! They're going to kill each other! Run! Get out of the way! Somebody get me my crutches! Jim, get away from them!"* No one brought Cartee his crutches, and Jim wouldn't get away from the dog fight.

While the rest of us were grabbing children and scrambling for cover (except broken Cartee, who curled into a ball on his blanket), Jim was trying to stop the attack. He would first grab one dog and then the other, trying to throw the dog he was holding far enough away from the other one to stop the fight. The problem was that each dog he had was being bitten by the other one, so the "throw" included both of them each time. Again and again, Jim was grabbing and pitching, grabbing and pitching, trying to work the fighting dogs to the river, which was about 30 feet away. The growling, screaming, running, and throwing continued until just before Jim and the dogs reached the water. Our dog Sarge took a fierce bite to her throat from Bo and dropped to a submissive pose. Bo immediately stopped fighting, walked over to Sarge, stared at her for a minute, and then started licking Sarge's wounds. (Neither dog had suffered any serious injuries. The bleeding stopped quickly, and we were able to treat their bites effectively with the pet care kits we both had.)

But there was no licking Jim's wounds. During the fight, Jim received one bite on his thigh and two on his butt. Even worse, his pride was seriously wounded. He could not believe that he couldn't stop the fight. *"I thought it was a fair fight. There's 200 pounds of dog and I'm 200 pounds—even match. I didn't figure on all those legs! I thought I could stop them. I thought that even if a Bengal tiger attacked me, I could fight him off! But I can't. If a Bengal tiger attacked me—I'd die!"* (I'm not sure why Jim was anticipating a Bengal tiger attack in southeast Missouri.)

Jim refused treatment for his bites—probably as a way of punishing himself for having "lost the fight." After a few weeks and large doses of antibiotics for the infection that ensued because he wouldn't let us minister to his wounds, Jim was physically fine. But to this day, the memory of the great dog fight and the completely unexpected "loss" remains.

The **Life Lesson** is this: *If you are going to walk right into something, you want to know about and be prepared for all aspects of it—the good, the bad, and the ugly. What you encounter could have a lot of "legs."*

Be Ready for What You Ask For

At some point, it will become clear to you from the reactions of others that *"this must be what I'm going to be when I grow up—a leader!"* Real leaders' realization and acknowledgement of their skills always comes much later to them than it does to others. People who announce, *"I'm going to be a great leader,"* and receive looks of surprise or disbelief from others, are likely not emerging leaders. They are wanna-bes. The wanna-bes have somehow determined that being a leader is a "premier" position with lots of benefits, and few or no downsides, so that's what they want to be. I have witnessed this occurrence several times while teaching leadership skills. This is also something that is not gender-specific. Both men and women can go down this egocentric and likely (for them) attainable path. *Pink Leadership* may not be for those people, although this particular topic may be—be prepared for what you ask for!

Regardless of the industry or work environment where you eventually focus your attention, if you are to become a real leader, at the core of who you are is leadership. You may be a customer service manager, CIO, project leader, union steward, school principal (or teacher), entrepreneur, politician, or the head of your local United Way charity drive. Wherever and in whatever professional areas your talents are applied, you have grown up to be a leader. At the point when your leadership skills are obvious to you, you have the privilege of making a decision: Do you want to continue to develop as a leader and expand your sphere of influence, or would you be more comfortable confining your skills to a more limited and more known environment? It's your call—make it a conscious call.

If you simply drift into focusing your leadership attention one way or the other, you will not be as effective because your heart and your energy are likely not fully committed. You may not be prepared for what you're asking for. When all the "legs" come at you in your quest to be a leader—you may want to just curl up in a ball and holler for someone to bring your crutches. Instead, recognize that you are a leader and choose to apply your skills in the most appropriate arena for you. There are people who chose to focus their leadership skills on a "local" level, such as home, the PTA, or their chosen charitable groups. This decision can make a substantial, positive contribution to all people and organizations that receive the benefit of the leader's talents. (Leadership is not only required in a boardroom. It's also a necessity for a successful Girl Scout cookie drive.) Other leaders will choose to expand and apply their skills to a professional environment in an almost unlimited array of business fields.

When I need to choose between different options for...just about anything about which I have little personal knowledge, I seek out the people who have information about the different choices I've identified. I might ask, *"What is the worst thing about vacationing in Cabo San Lucas, and what did you like least about Maui?"* I've already read the tourist brochures. I know what is touted as the wonderfulness of each place. What are the bad points? If I can accept the bad, I'm already certain I can accept the good!

That's why *Pink Leadership* begins with the less-than-wonderful aspects of being a leader. You probably already know the benefits. If you also know the bad points, and are willing to accept those, you are making a fully informed decision. Am I trying to discourage you from wanting to be a leader? Not at all. Nor are you being "sold" on leadership. You must already have the drive for leadership because you're reading this book. Leadership is a long and often difficult quest. You will want to recognize the realities of a leadership position to minimize surprises that could cause you to fail in your leadership decision. If we don't know that a marathon is 26 miles before we sign up, we may be very sorry we've started the run and give up before the end, or at the least, we may run very, very slowly and painfully. Being a good leader means being prepared to "go the distance."

Being a superior leader is not all recognition and applause and a host of people eager to take direction and follow you. There are a few less-than-savory aspects of leadership that are often discounted or swept under the rug. The noted author James Baldwin said, *"The price one pays for pursuing any profession or calling is an intimate knowledge of its ugly side."* In the interest of full disclosure, the lessons contained in *Pink Leadership* start by getting you more intimate with the ugly side of leadership. We'll go to the dark side first. There are fewer surprises down the road that way!

My Grandpa Tony[8] taught me, *"You can't fight the devil until you stand up and look him in the eyes."* (For authenticity, you should read this quote with a heavy Italian accent.) Having the courage to "look the devil in the eyes" is the first step to avoiding the surprise when the dark side appears.

Because of the complexity and desirability of being a leader, there are actually several devils lurking on the periphery of leadership. These devils may try to discourage you, throw you off course, or even sabotage your success at being a leader. By knowing the devils' names and recognizing them for the distractions that they are when they rear their ugly heads, you will take a significant step in casting them aside.

The devils' names are as follows:

- ► Pyrite Devil
- ► Chatter Devil
- ► Precious Devil
- ► OCD Devil

---

[8] My grandfather, Tony Pecchia, immigrated to the United States in 1913 when he was 24 years old. He came from a small farming community in Italy on the top of a mountain just south of Rome. Despite his lack of formal education, he was one of the wisest men I've ever known. He was also an excellent listener!

CHAPTER 2

Throw Away the Fool's Gold

THERE WAS (AND maybe still is) an unscrupulous practice when potential gold mine owners wanted to sell a mine. They would "salt the mine" with iron pyrite, commonly known as fool's gold. Blasting the sides of the already dug tunnels in the mine with gold-like sparkle would substantially increase the perceived value, and subsequently the price, of the mine.

We can also be tricked by fool's gold. When we are looking at what is required of a real leader, and what makes up superior leadership, we may be blinded by the glitter and end up covered in cheap pyrite. In order to differentiate between all sparkle and real leadership gold, we need to know what we're looking for. If we don't, we can be led down the wrong path by the Pyrite Devil.

Life Lesson #3: Violins and the Brass...
and a Few Renegade Oboes

My husband Bill has a strong appreciation for classical music. I, on the other hand, don't understand why someone listens to anything that you can't sing along with or dance to. In the interest of a peaceful co-existence, Vivaldi and funky Motown alternate on our CD changer.

A few years ago, I arrived home from a difficult day at Nordstrom (shopping, not working) to find Bill sitting on the edge of his chair listening to his latest classical music purchase.

"Jeanne, you really need to listen to this—it's incredible!"

I sat down wearily, managed a small "gee-I'm-really-excited" smile, and resigned myself to hearing...whatever "incredible" thing was playing. Bill re-started the song, settled back in his chair, and closed his eyes in satisfied concentration. I assumed the same position, figuring that at least I could get a short nap in. Too quickly, Bill leaned forward and exclaimed, *"Did you hear that? Did you hear the way the violins were challenging the brass! That was just extraordinary!"*

My expression could best be described as a deer in the headlights. Challenging the brass? Yeah, sure, I heard that. I expected a fight to break out any minute! What does "challenging the brass" mean? How did he hear that?

A few months later, we were attending a classical concert at the Orange County, California, Performing Arts Center. (I do take the "peaceful co-existence" approach seriously.) I was actually enjoying the performance (because they were playing a syncopated piece that sounded a lot like hip-hop to me) when Bill winced noticeably. During the intermission, I asked what caused his reaction.

His reply was, "*Those oboes really let the conductor down.*" Violins and the brass, and now oboes—what was I missing, and why? I spent the rest of the concert thinking about why he could hear so easily what I could not hear at all.

My conclusion was that Bill truly understands what he's hearing when it comes to classical music. He has a refined perspective of "good" and "not-so-good." His quality standards are higher than mine because he has listened to and studied the best in the field and he knows what to look for. He selected his examples of quality well. I would have chosen the Pyrite Devil with the hip-hop rhythm as the best, whereas Bill winced at this performance when "the oboes really let the conductor down."

I knew I had learned a valuable Life Lesson: *If you want to achieve something, learn all you can about it so that you make the right decisions about the good, the bad, and how to get to where you want to be.*

Don't Settle for "Okay"—Go for the Gold!

The Pyrite Devil appears in several disguises all through our lives to deliver his false messages of how to be a superior leader. He shows us nothing more than fool's gold, however. Because the Devil's particular "talent" is in falsehood, he can easily prevent us from recognizing that he's there in the spoken words, print, and pictures that try to throw us off course. The Pyrite Devil has two goals:

1. Confuse you about "how you should be"—give poor or wrong guidelines about how a woman should act to succeed.

2. Offer up "false gods"—the wrong role model or the right role model for the wrong reasons.

Let's look at the first goal. The Pyrite Devil will throw up smoke-screens and spout falsehoods that lead you to believe that women should:

► Always agree with their leaders and certainly never "stir things up"—even when they know they're right and that something needs stirring. We are encouraged by the Pyrite Devil to confide in a man, and after getting his buy-in, allow him to lead any challenges. Women are not supposed to "cause trouble." (That certainly keeps us in our place— quietly supportive and living behind the curtain!)

► Avoid spending too much visible time with other women (particularly at work). We certainly shouldn't be seen as "one of the girls." (This will effectively cut off our information sources and thought-processing opportunities with other bright women. One woman alone is easy "to deal with." But a whole passel of them? That's too hard to handle! Divide us and someone else will conquer!)

► Always volunteer for or accept graciously the assignments that are "a woman's job." This includes bringing in the lunch for the working meeting, shopping for the right paper and presentation materials for the big demo coming up, and calling 30 people on the list to remind them about the big event—that someone else is planning and leading. (Doing these things is not bad if we actually want and choose to. However, if we're **always** doing the women's work, we don't have time to work on the "good stuff." The Devil doesn't mention that we can and should do some of each—the take-care-of-logistics tasks and the leadership jobs too.)

▶ Be nice and get along with others all the time. (More about "nice" is coming up.) We are supposed to be "the gentler sex." (I hear you growling over that one! But you know the irritating descriptor and all it implies still hovers over us.)

▶ Make sure that they never raise their voices in either excitement or dismay, or joy or anger. A loud woman is just too scary. We need to demonstrate that we are under control of ourselves and our emotions at all times, so that others don't have to figure out how to deal with expressions of how we feel. (Many men are unsure of how to deal with their wives or partners how-I-feel expressions at home. They certainly don't want to have to try to get it right at work. Of course, bottling our feelings up until they erupt (often too strongly and at not the best time) reinforces that we just aren't "stable enough" for leadership.)

▶ Never cry. To cry or not—that is the question. You have heard and read both, "It's okay," and, "Never, ever let them see you cry." There are two problems with not crying.

   1. If you are a "crier," you will spend all your thinking time and energy trying to stop yourself from doing it. You won't be able to focus on whatever discussion or situation has made you want to cry. (And your eyes and nose may get really red and give you away anyway...and you'll look terrible.)

   2. If you effectively prevent yourself from crying right then when you need to, you may have just delayed the reaction. Later on, when something happens that may not be worth crying over—that's when you'll cry. It just comes spilling out because it's leftover from

the last go around. Then the crying seems really inappropriate because it is.

There are two problems with crying.

1. It may happen too often, and once you start, you may have a problem stopping. There are definitely some things that are worth crying over—like ugly things happening directly to you or to other people. If you are really sad because Liz is getting laid off (or because you are!), then a few tears are warranted. But things that happen to "things" like process changes, plans gone awry, or losing your notes on the way to your presentation—they just aren't worth it. They are only "things." The challenge for a crier is to learn to compartmentalize—to know what's worth crying over and say, *"Oh well, that's really frustrating"* to all the rest and move on. Learning to cry appropriately is a skill worth working on!

2. People around you don't know how to deal with it. Then you'll feel bad for them, and you'll do whatever you feel has to be done to make that person feel better, and then you'll be upset on several levels. You're already upset over whatever made you cry, and now you're concerned about your crying-viewer's feelings. This is just too much strain on you, may enhance your need to cry, and is an inappropriate distraction.

Did you know that an "appeal to sympathy" from women is taught to some salespeople—specifically car salesmen? If you express unhappiness with the "great deal" you've been offered and imply (or state directly) that you feel you are being tricked or ripped off, the instruction in a sales training book I read, is: *"Tell the woman buyer that you are really hurt because she's implied that you are not telling her the truth. Mention several times how bad you feel. Diffuse her anger by diverting it into sympathy for you."*

My take on "To cry or not to cry" is—cry when you are supposed to. If you can excuse yourself and cry alone, that's even better. But if you can't escape for a little private crying time…oh well, just get it over with where you are as quickly as you can. However, do not believe that you own the other person's inability to handle your sadness. It is not your fault if someone else doesn't know what to do. You don't have to fix that too. A quick, *"Sorry about that,"* is good enough. Move on. The Pyrite Devil will tell you that if you **ever** cry, you have just shot yourself in the foot for current or future career opportunities. The Devil says that because he doesn't know how to handle a woman's tears.

I say a "woman's tears" as though women are the only ones who cry at work, which is so not true. In my roles as a strategist and an executive coach, I'm often discussing angst-inducing topics with clients. Some of those topics are worth crying over, and the clients do—both the women and the men. I have personally seen almost as many men cry as I have women. I was teaching a class in consulting skills to a group of bright professional men and women and the issue of clients' emotional responses came up. Somehow we wandered into the "crying" area. I said what I just wrote, *"I have personally seen as many men cry as I have women."* What a response that statement elicited from the group! The women said nothing—they just smiled and gave barely perceptible nods. But the men were horrified, completely disbelieving, and very vocal about it. *"What? Are you serious? Men crying at work? No way! I can't believe that!"* I knew that many of them knew better. Their reaction was both self-protecting and a cover-up. Those men didn't want to believe that a man cries at work because if they believe it can happen—then it could happen to them! Oh, the horror of it all!

One of the men asked, *"What are you doing to make them cry?"* I replied that I didn't **make** them cry, I **let** them cry. He said, *"Well, I want you to call me the next time that happens. No matter where you are, I'm going there! I want to see this for myself!"* The next time it happened was less than a month later, in Madrid, Spain. (I didn't call him to come there.)

My boss, Paul (the head of our consulting practice), and I went to Madrid because we had a seriously challenged project going on. The client was dissatisfied, our team was unhappy, and the project was stalled. Paul and I needed to find out what had gone wrong and then determine how to get everyone happier and everything back on track. In our first hour at the client site, we knew this was a very emotionally-charged situation when the executive sponsor was screaming at us (literally) and banging his fist on the table. The sponsor could barely speak because his mouth was so full of our butts! This was not going to go down easily.

After the first meeting, we were scheduled for three full days of talking to all the project principals. Going into our designated meeting room, I stopped Paul and asked him to grab a box of Kleenex to leave in our room. I said, *"There will be some crying going on in there this week."* He stared wide-eyed at me—not wanting to believe but afraid not to. He grabbed the Kleenex and brought it with us.

On the second afternoon of the meetings, we were having a long and extremely difficult conversation with the client's warehouse director who I'll call Jose. The conversation was more difficult because we were all challenged by language. Jose spoke mostly Spanish with some poor English mixed in. I spoke mostly English with some poor Spanish and a little Italian when I couldn't think of the words in Spanish. Paul only spoke English—so he wasn't ever really in the discussion. An hour into the meeting, Jose told me something that was worth crying about and he cried. Jose cried, I was quiet, and Paul stared at the desk. Paul had not followed the topic, but he knew crying when he saw it! He passed the Kleenex box to me, and I handed it off to Jose. And we went on.

Thirty minutes later, we left the meeting. We had talked through a possible work-around for the problem, Jose felt better, I was relieved that I didn't have to struggle for the words any longer, and Paul was still in shock. *"What happened in there? He was crying! I never saw **that** before!"* My reply was, *"Welcome to my world. This is how it really happens when people feel safe enough to be real."* I then told him what Jose had told me, and Paul agreed that it was worth crying over. Paul never again ignored the truth that men would (or should) cry occasionally. In fact, a few times over the ensuing years, he would tell me when he was in a conversation with a man who cried. I was always very proud of Paul in these situations—it meant that he was making the other person feel safe enough to be real.

Beware of the False Gods

The second goal of the Pyrite Devil is to offer up "false gods"—the wrong role model or the right role model for the wrong reasons. We're going to explore the arena of role models in just a few more pages in this chapter. Keep reading.

In order to prevent the Pyrite Devil from achieving his goals and throwing us off course, we need to know what the course is—what path does a "real gold" leader take. There may be born leaders, but you are not just born knowing exactly **how** to develop and apply the skills of a leader. The foundational characteristics of a good leader are both genetic and environmentally developed. You already read the list of leadership characteristics in the first chapter. Let's revisit them. Good leaders are born with the characteristics that would lead them to be the following:

- ► Enthusiastic and passionate
- ► Trustworthy and honest
- ► Authentic and respectful in their approach to others
- ► Comfortable and calm with change or ambiguity
- ► Confident
- ► Brave

To make sure that we're all singing from the same hymnal, I'm not saying that at the moment of conception we are enthusiastic and passionate, trustworthy and honest, and all those other qualities on the list. However, there are underlying, genetic traits that we are born with that lay the groundwork for us to become enthusiastic, passionate, trustworthy...and all the others. We are then trained, prodded, cajoled, guided, and coached into the leadership characteristics.

How do you use congenital traits that were nurtured and encouraged by parents, family members, teachers, or someone else to then develop the skills and abilities that you need to be a real gold leader? Getting from Point A (the innate and environmentally-enhanced characteristics) to Point B (the development of the knowledge and abilities to deliver leadership skills) requires:

- ► Listening with our ears and eyes
- ► Learning from wherever it comes
- ► Perfect practice
- ► Finding the right role models

Listening With Our Ears and Eyes

You have already read about the significance that **listening** has to a leader in the first chapter of this book. You cannot practice what you have not learned and you cannot learn what you have not listened to—with your ears and eyes. Listening is the starting point in developing the leadership skills you're seeking. Listening is so important that we should re-visit the Chapter 1 commentary on listening again.

No one person has all the answers to the challenges we face in life and in business. There are, of course, the obvious benefits of listening: gathering significant data and receiving different perspectives to resolve problems. However, related to the ability to lead, listening is a demonstration to others that you value their input, are carefully weighing all options, and as a consequence, you can be trusted to make the right decisions. One of the simpler definitions among the 726,000 Google choices for leadership is, "Having followers." We all want and need to be listened to. A leader who provides the opportunity for us to be heard is the person we are apt to believe in and follow. My conclusion, from my own experience and from observing and listening to others, is, "If we do not listen well, we will not lead well."

Listening, with your ears and your eyes, is the key to your development into a superior leader. Complex leadership skill sets, with the willingness and ability to apply them, are unique to each individual. You can admire and try to emulate great leaders, but you cannot provide leadership in the exact way they do. You cannot do exactly the same things. You are not the same person. Listen to others and then personalize, practice, and perfect your own skills. Learn to recognize and develop your personal characteristics of leadership—working with others toward a common goal. Never walk with your head empty. Listen—listen over and over and over again.

(Here's the part I promised you about being nice.) The good news for women is that we are trained to be good listeners—although not exactly for the best (or only) reasons. The primary reason that we are taught to listen is because it's the polite thing to do…and it's nice. Girls (women) are told that we are supposed to be nice. We are encouraged, taught, and coached to be nice because girls (women) are supposed to be liked. (Yes, males also expect and are expected to be liked. However, for females, this is a very big issue, as you already know!) People like other people who are nice—therefore, girls (women) are supposed to be nice. If boys (men) are nice, then it's a bonus. "Niceness" isn't as high on the list of requirements for males as it is for females. And we learn this almost from infancy!

Picture this. A two-year-old boy named Todd and a girl named Heather are playing together for the first time. If Heather runs over to Todd and hugs and kisses him, we say, *"Yes, what a nice little girl you are!"* If Todd initiates the kissing (or even if he kisses back), we say, *"Oh, look at what he did! Todd is such a good little boy!"* We comment on Todd's affection with delight and some surprise. Because we're really expecting Todd to hit Heather over the head with his toy truck or push her down, mid-hug. If Todd does what we expect, and Heather is flat on her butt, we say, *"Todd, don't do that! Be nice to Heather!"* And then one of us turns to the other mother and says with a smile, *"That Todd is sure all boy, isn't he?"* Now, just what is the message there?

The more female-focused "play nice" mandates become listening lessons as we get older. *"If you want a boy (man) to like you, listen to him."* Your mother, sisters, and friends, Teen Magazine, and Cosmo all told you this. That's what being nice is as we get older. But should we listen to be liked…because it's the nice thing to do? The teaching is good—we must learn to listen—but the primary reason of being perceived as nice is not so good when we get outside of our social fences. Remember my sister-in-law Toni from the first chapter? She's the great listener that everyone wants to sit by and talk to. Yes, we like her, but we gravitate towards her because she listens. One of the requirements of being a leader is to have followers. Listen and they will come. That's the reason a leader listens—to learn and to have others follow and learn from her—not because she wants to be nice.

"Nice" is such a terrible word! It means pleasant or pleasing or agreeable. Those are such namby-pamby adjectives! Nice may be okay socially, but it doesn't cut it for leadership. Leaders are not necessarily nice, and lots of good leaders are not even liked. (However, the Pyrite Devil is nice so that he can suck you in to believing his lies.) Although all good leaders may not be liked, they are all respected. They are respected because they are courteous and respectful, empathetic and compassionate. They are kind. But they are not always very "pleasant, pleasing, or agreeable." It's possible that we use the word "nice" to describe someone because we don't know another word. It's time to learn a new one. How about "kind"? Kind means: having or showing a tender and considerate and helpful nature; used especially of persons and their behavior. Kind is a better word—it's a leader's word.

Women also develop the ability to listen with our ears and eyes early on because we like to know everything and we are prolific information-sharers. That incredible ability to repeat conversations verbatim, with all the accompanying visual details, is a skill we learn from the time we are young girls. Our mothers, older sisters, and friends want to know everything that happened and every word that was said. We learn to listen at a very early age because we're expected to repeat what we've heard and seen. We've heard the following from our female relatives and companions:

► *"No, not just 'okay.' Tell me **exactly** what your father said."*
► *"So, **exactly** what did he say about me?"*

►*"She said **what**? What did she look like? Was she smiling or...what?"*

►*"Just how did he start that ugly conversation? What did he say **exactly**?"*

Again, here's the good news. Since the development of the knowledge and abilities to deliver leadership skills requires listening with our ears and eyes—women have a leg up on this characteristic. For whatever reason, women are taught and learn to listen. If you are a man reading *Pink Leadership*, you may begin to feel unjustly excluded from this section, and possibly a few others that are coming up. Are you thinking, *"Now just wait a minute. I've been taught this too. I know how to listen. I have lots of the skills that you're saying are owned by women."* If you are one of those men, identify yourself. Raise your hand. (We'll take a short pause here, while I wait for your hand to go up.) Okay, I see you now—and I salute you! Now, while you are justifiably feeling good about yourself, look around. Do you see a crowd of other men around you with their hands in the air? I don't think so. You, and some other men, have the skills (and issues) that I call out as female-specific. However, I'm speaking in generalizations—most women and most men. If your hand is in the air, then you are not in the category of "most men." And, for what *Pink Leadership* is about—that's a good thing. Pat yourself on the back with your other hand.

Learning From Wherever It Comes

Now, we'll move to the second component in the development of leadership skills: **learning from wherever it comes.** The necessity of learning as a significant leadership development requirement is a given. Moving from "how you are" to "what you will do well" requires knowing what to do with what you are and what you have. As an example: If you are authentic and calm and brave, you have the basis for conflict resolution. Conflict resolution is an applied ability that is one of the hallmarks of a superior leader. Without learning the techniques you need to employ for different types of conflicts and people, however, you may not actually be able to apply "how you are" very well.

Here's another bit of good news for women. We are prolific learners! We are trained to learn about things that we do not even care about. One of the reasons why we learn about so many things is because we need to do so many different things. Another reason we are taught to learn so early on in our development from toddler to girl to woman goes back to being liked...and nice. We learn (again from mothers, sisters, friends, and magazines) that, *"He'll ask you out again if you talk about what he's interested in."* (I personally spent a lot of time reading and learning about engine sizes, carburetors, and exhaust systems when I was 16 years old—because cars were kings then!) So, we actively learn about cars or fishing, hockey or football so that we can listen to him explain it to us again, and ask the right questions that show we care about all those things. Does that work both ways? Are little boys coached to learn about fashion, dance, art, or cooking so that their dates will want to go out with them again? That would be no. If the conversation turned to, *"Do you think that navy blue is going to be a hot color for fall?"* just watch that guy shut down! That's "girl talk." He has no need to learn about that stuff.

Concurrently, we are learning, learning, learning all the things we have to know to survive as women. We have to learn how to tape (or staple) up the hem of a too-long dress right before we're walking out the door. We have to learn how to apply makeup in the dark. (You know why.) We have to learn to fold fitted sheets. These are some of the small learning requirements. (Small but not insignificant when your hem is down or your makeup is smeared in the dark.) Then there are the major learning requirements—birthing and parenting. Yes, our husbands/partners or some other male may accompany us to those classes. But who signs up for them and pays the most attention because they know they **seriously** need to know that stuff! Women do! We have to deliver on the birthing and parenting knowledge—literally and figuratively.

Women are learners. We are always forging new ground—we read, we watch, we ask...and we learn. We have another leg up on the development of the knowledge and abilities to deliver leadership skills—learning from wherever it comes. We're just not that specific about our learning opportunities—we turn down few of them.

> As part of my responsibility to provide leadership and management training in my "day job," I recently offered an excellent self-study book on effective meeting skills to our company managers. I got immediate, *"Great! Thanks! Please send it to me!"* responses from all the female managers. One of the male managers said, *"No, don't send it to me. I probably won't have time to read it."* From the other men, I received no response at all. Turn down a free book? Decline an opportunity to learn something? I thought this was interesting...not surprising...but certainly interesting.

Perfect Practice

Successful application of innate traits requires listening, learning... and practice. Many people appear to believe that all that is required to perfect any skill is to **practice** it. Practice alone does not make perfect. Perfect practice makes perfect—knowing what to practice and then doing it the right way. I have taught presentation skills to hundreds of executives, consultants, sales personnel, and emerging leaders in five countries for the past seventeen years. I have heard several times, *"I don't really think I need this class. I've been doing presentations for years, so I've had lots of practice."* In all those years, I have seen three people for whom this statement was true. They really did not need the class. They had practiced, and subsequently developed and refined, perfect technique. The other hundreds of people—not so good. They may have practiced for years, but they had not practiced perfectly. Unfortunately, they had locked in poor (and in some cases, really bad) technique and they did not present well. But they thought they did. Some of these people were real emerging leaders, and they listened and were able to correct their years of poor practice. Some of them were in the grips of the Precious Devil that you will meet in Chapter 4. They chose not to listen, learn, and then practice perfectly. They didn't have to. They believed they were superior leaders. They already knew everything they needed to know.

Did the "know-everything-twice-already" attitude people brought to the presentation class negatively affect any of them? Absolutely! In one case that I witnessed, there was a direct and immediate career impact. For several years, I taught professional skills as part of a ten-week leadership training program for a major international software company in their corporate university in the Netherlands. At the conclusion of a presentation workshop, the president of the company attended the final presentations to *"find his super-stars."* One of the "I-already-know-how-to-do-this" attendees (who needs to remain nameless) presented very poorly in his final speech, as he had likely done in all presentations he'd ever given. After the class, the president asked the participant, and me, about his experience attending the workshop. The participant's response was, *"I really didn't have anything to learn. I already know how to do this, so it was a waste of my time to attend this class."* Certainly, what he was also implying to the president was, *"And you have wasted your money in sending me here."* The president immediately corrected his own mistake in hiring the individual. His reply to the participant was, *"If you believe that you have nothing to learn, then you are not a leader for my company. You should pack your bags. I will have a driver take you to the airport. You will not be attending the rest of our program."* All negative impacts will not be as swift or as dramatic as this example, but eventually, the unwillingness to listen, learn, and practice will reveal the real person—just a wanna-be leader.

In contrast, I saw a woman who put herself at risk in front of her colleagues and peers to be able to practice perfectly to achieve what she wanted. I was teaching a Train the Trainer class that included several video-taped opportunities for the attendees to practice their presentation and teaching styles and skills. One of the participants from this large pharmaceutical company was a female accountant who I'll call Susan. Susan had been very quiet the first day, although her body language said that she was totally engaged and focused on the class. I gave the assignment and told the class that they would have the opportunity to present their material two times the next day. They would view their videos and receive immediate feedback from me and from their colleagues. I said we would be simulating an actual working environment for them. There were the usual groans and please-don't-make-me-do-this looks from several of the participants, but not from Susan. I saw her nod her head slowly and smile.

The next morning, they all arrived looking the way they did the day before—dressed in something much less than "business casual." (Attending internal classes in this company was a license to wear jeans and t-shirts.) All but one looked like they were on their way to wash their cars right after work. Not Susan—she looked spectacular! She was wearing a gorgeous business suit, professional (polished) heels, and perfectly appropriate makeup, and she had obviously spent a lot of time doing her hair! Everyone commented on how great Susan looked. (One guy whistled—how rude!) Someone asked, *"Susan, why did you get so dressed up?"* Her reply was a great learning experience! *"I may not get another chance to practice just the way I want to do it. I want to try it and to see myself do it perfectly."* There was dead silence while the others hung their heads. I couldn't have paid for a better answer than that! After pausing to make sure they were absorbing what Susan had just taught them, I initiated the applause that they all joined in on. When it was her turn to present, Susan was letter-perfect! She totally rocked! (A year later, I received a call from Susan. She told me that one of the reasons she had tried so hard in the class was that she really wanted to work toward a career in training. She wanted me to know that she had just received a promotion to the Director of Training and Development for her company. You go, girl!)

Finding the Right Role Models

We have now come to the last element in the leadership litany of listening, learning, perfect practice, and **finding the right role models**. We need standards to follow, examples to emulate, and patterns of accomplishment to strive for. The arena of role models is loaded with Pyrite Devils!

Choosing the right role models for you implies that you know how to evaluate and determine the good from the not-even-close-to-good. This sounds like an easy task, until you actually have to examine why you want to be a leader. What kind of a leader will you be? What will be the outcomes of your leadership? After you answer these initial questions, query further to identify your perfect role models. Why would a particular person be a good role model for you? What traits do they possess that you want to develop? What do they do that makes you say, *"I want to be like her (or him)"*? What have they accomplished that you want to imitate? If you don't ask these questions, and carefully listen to your own answers, you may wind up in the clutches of the Pyrite Devil. You may be blinded by the false sparkle. The pyrite may lead you in the wrong direction or cloud your vision, and subsequently, your achievement of superior leadership.

Throughout our lives, we are asked, *"Who is your hero?"* (Read: role model.) This is a standard homework assignment during grade school, middle school, and high school. (I don't remember being asked this in college, however. Maybe my professors just didn't care—or figured that we would all automatically respond with their names!) We read or hear the answers to this question from celebrities, corporate and world leaders, and "the man on the street," in magazines, on the Internet, and in television programs. Sometimes the responses are, at the least, intriguing or, at the worst, frightening!

> When my insightful and beautiful granddaughter, Carissa Alicea, was in the seventh grade, she told me about her assignment of "Who is your hero?" She was obviously concerned about the marked difference between her response and the answers of some others in her class. She said, *"Meme, lots of kids in my class picked people like Britney Spears and Justin Timberlake. Do you think that's right?"* I didn't answer her question directly, but instead asked whom she had selected. Her hero was Rosa Parks. I asked why Rosa Parks was her hero. Her answer was, *"Because she did what she believed in, even if it was hard."* I asked why she thought others picked celebrity heroes. Carissa wasn't sure, but offered that maybe because they were beautiful, famous, and rich. I asked which she'd rather be—beautiful, famous, and rich or someone who does what they believe in, even it if is hard? She thought it over briefly, smiled, and nodded her head in understanding of what she was hearing. *"Rosa Parks."* Carissa had already asked herself the important questions about her own role models; she just didn't realize that she had gone through that thought process. Carissa knew how to select her role model—she was not going to be caught by the celebrity-status Pyrite Devils.

The thought-process questions that will allow you to pick a "real gold" role model are as follows:

> ▶ Why do I want to be a leader? Is it for money, fame, and power, to do good or save the world, or just because I can?

- ► What skills and abilities do I want to learn and employ to be the kind of leader that I want to be?
- ► Who demonstrates the best of those leadership skills?
- ► Who do I want to be like?

If your reason to become a leader is for money, your role model may be Meg Whitman, the former president of eBay, or Donald Trump. If you want fame or power, your model may be any of the U.S. presidents. Do-good models could be Mother Theresa, or Ralph Nader, or the untiring head of your local homeless shelter.

A mistake that some militant feminists or insecure men make is to confine their role-model list to their own gender. This choice is really unfortunate and eliminates some excellent candidates. Watch, listen to, study, learn from, and emulate the best—regardless of their sex.

To help jump-start your thinking about your own list, I'll share some of my role models with you. My list of role models is long, and it continues to grow as I understand more of my needs and discover new people to admire and emulate. Interestingly, no one has ever been taken off my list once they've been added.

My "real gold" role models include some "staples" in role modeling such as the following:

- ► Martha Stewart for her incredible energy and wisdom in building a successful empire by amassing around her the best people in their respective fields.

- ► Oprah Winfrey for believing in her model of helping people to grow spiritually, emotionally, and intellectually when her television producers did not share her vision. And for making it happen!

Both of these women are also wealthy and they are celebrities. However, they made my list for what they've done for the reasons that I value. (I'm not saying that I would ever turn down rich and famous—but that isn't why I choose to be a leader.)

My unique-to-me role model list is longer and more varied. It includes the following:

▶ My husband, Bill Gulbranson, who consistently shows his respect for the individuality, humanity, and unique contributions of everyone he meets. An example of his respectfulness is that he notices, remembers, and uses in conversation the names of waitresses, valets, airport bag checkers, and the entire rest of the world! Once, when I asked why he does this, he told me, *"Because each person should be recognized for being a valuable person."* I want to be that kind of leader.

▶ Milton Frenzel, who lived in my small home town and who is one of the most intelligent men I have ever known. While I admired his intelligence, however, he didn't make my role model list on the basis of what he knew. Mr. Frenzel is one of my role models because of his consistent willingness to share his knowledge with others (including me as a teenager) in a way that made the learner believe they had done him a favor by asking for his help. There was no "shame" in needing Mr. Frenzel's help. He made others believe that helping them was a gift to him. Mr. Frenzel is my model for selfless support and kindness. I want to be that kind of leader.

▶ My daughter, Julie LeGrand, is the best mother I've ever known. She genuinely revels in both the positive and the less-than-thrilling aspects of being a mother and is willing to do whatever is required to raise her children well. She embraces both the good and the bad aspects of her role with equal enthusiasm and joy. It's unfortunate (for both Julie and for me) that she was not available to be my role model when I was "mothering" her! I want to be a leader who brings joy to others.

There is a special category of role models—the role model's model. I have been fortunate to work with a man who consciously and consistently demonstrates the best attributes of a role model and mentor and subsequently the abilities of a superior leader. My personal model for role-modeling is Bob Dickey.[9] Bob's career path and mine have been intertwined in interesting ways for the last 15+ years. Sometimes I have worked for Bob, sometimes he has worked for me, and sometimes we have worked as colleagues and peers. I knew that he would be my model for role-modeling from the first time I worked with him. I saw then, and continue to see now, Bob's willingness and ability to demonstrate his firm belief that "the role of a supervisor (leader) is to identify the roadblocks to a person's success, and then work diligently to remove them." He recognizes that to support others he first needs to foster in them the drive to want to excel in whatever it is they're doing. Because he understands that most people need benchmarks and standards to measure themselves, Bob conscientiously, and without complaint, does what is required and expected of him. He provides the visible model of working hard, which encourages others to follow his lead. When his followers are willing to work hard themselves, Bob preemptively looks for roadblocks in their success paths and works tirelessly to remove them. This may include more training or coaching, a whisper (or a shout) in the ear of an even higher up, a new process to follow, or reaching out to another person who is willing and able to

---

[9] Bob has held a number of impressive and responsible positions in his career in the information systems arena. His titles have included Director, Vice-President, and Strategist. Regardless of his titles, Bob's approach has been the same: modeling hard work and supporting others to achieve their successes.

help his people. Bob does what role models (and leaders) should do. I have personally benefited and grown in my own ability to be a good role model for others just by watching what Bob does and then following his lead. Look for your Bob Dickey (whether he turns out to be a man or a woman), and when you identify him or her, watch, listen, and learn.

You will also likely end up with a long list of staple and unique role models. When you know what superior leadership qualities include, and you know why you want to be a leader, you will be able to know who you want to emulate and learn from. You will be able to evade the Pyrite Devil. You will not allow yourself to be led down the wrong path to leadership.

CHAPTER 3

Don't Be Surprised by the Noise

THE SECOND LEADERSHIP devil causes everyone to want to know your business. There will be lots of chattering about you. People you don't know and have never even heard of will spend time and effort discussing and dissecting what you do, or what they imagine you do. Depending on your sphere of influence and exposure, you will be the subject of water-cooler chatter, e-mail gossip trails, dinner party conversation, and/or sensational media coverage. Your life and actions will become more interesting to others just because you are a leader. That's the Chatter Devil. Let's look him in the eye.

Life Lesson #4: Bread, Butter, and Jelly People

I spent much of my life, and started my own family, in a town of 1,500 people. (If you have always lived in an urban setting and have longed for the "simpler life," this story also provides a slightly jaundiced take on one of the less-than-delightful aspects of small-town living

When there is not much of interest going on in a small town (and that is often the case), most conversations revolve around the small details of what the residents are doing. I called it gossip.

My mother interpreted it as "taking an interest in people." Throughout the 17 years that I lived in that very small town, it appeared that too many people "took an interest" in me too often.

I was complaining about being the subject of local conversation to my children's 16-year-old babysitter (whose name I have forgotten), when she gave me a life lesson in the reality of being a leader.

"There are bread, butter, and jelly people. Most people are bread. They are the 'regular people'—mostly everyone on earth and, for sure, most of the people in town. They aren't particularly interesting—they just go on about their lives. You need lots of bread people.

Then there are butter people. Butter people are that little extra. They are beautiful or rich, or they have something that the bread people don't have. You don't NEED to have butter people, but they're at least more interesting to look at and talk about than bread people.

Then there are the jelly people. They actually DO things that the bread and butter people don't do. They are the ones we watch— just to see what they'll do next. Sometimes they do really bad things—like jam that's too old. That's when the jelly people are the most interesting. And sometimes, they do really good things. Then the rest of us—the bread and butter people—get to decide if we like what they're doing. Maybe we want to do it too. Or maybe we just want to criticize to make ourselves feel better. Either way— jelly people are looked at and talked about all the time.

You are a jelly person because you do interesting things. I remember when you picketed the library because they took some books that you said were important off the shelf. Then

EVERYBODY wanted those books! People listen to you and do what you want them to, most of the time. That means you're going to get talked about a lot. Just get over yourself and learn to live with it!"

Talk about a serious jolt of reality and wisdom from the babysitter! This is a Life Lesson to listen to: *If you aspire to be a leader (or if you just want to live in a small town), then be prepared for the "noise."*

Get Past the Noise About You

Time and talking have validated the babysitter's lesson. As a leader, you will be talked about, and not always from a flattering perspective.

The president of a company that I worked for about 20 years ago once asked me if I had repeated a story about his questionably-appropriate relationship with another member of his corporate staff. When I readily admitted that I had relayed the information, he was at first taken aback by my immediate admission. I'm sure he was surprised to hear that I had spread the tale because I was a member of the management staff and not an "average Josephine" who may not have understood the entire situation. He then asked why I would talk about him and his personal life. My reply was, *"It's just too good to pass up."* I agreed that it was not a professional or positive thing for me to do, but it was normal and natural, and the topic was just too tempting to ignore. I explained that few people care if a "regular" employee engages in a marginally-acceptable relationship, but the president of the company? Now, that's interesting! I told him the Bread, Butter, and Jelly story. I also apologized for my breach of professionalism and assured him that I would work on getting my "normal and natural" reaction to juicy gossip under control. The president listened quietly to the life lesson. His reply was thoughtful and a demonstration of superior leadership. He said, *"I wanted to ignore the implications of the impression I might make because of my position in the company. Thank you for the reminder."*

It's unfortunate that this person needs to remain nameless because, with his response, my estimation of his leadership skills and my desire to follow his direction increased exponentially! The president was willing to listen and to learn, even from a "lowly" director. He was accepting of the need to change something in himself to provide the leadership he had promised to deliver to the company. And he had the good sense to ask me to, *"Never do that again,"* before we ended our conversation.

Certainly, the Chatter Devil is ugliest when you are doing something you don't want others to find out about. We only have to read the news to bring out the Chatter Devil for public leaders. Is there a month that goes by without news of some government or corporate leader who is "throwing away the kingdom" for a few extra dollars or a few nights of illicit pleasure? (It's interesting to note that there are few female leaders who make the headlines with the same inappropriate and sometimes illegal sexual dalliances. An exception could be Queen Elizabeth I, but that "license" may have just come with the territory then.) It appears that these leaders didn't recognize that the Chatter Devil was out there before they engaged in their activities. They didn't realize that they would be gossip fodder. Maybe they should have looked that devil in the eye.

The whole arena of doing something you should not be doing is the worst because, in addition to being just wrong, eventually you will be caught by someone. That someone will then be sure to share the news with all the others. Your leadership will then be attacked or could even be killed by the Chatter Devil. You can likely think of a long list of political leaders who are no longer our leaders because they were caught doing what they should not have been. (It's interesting to note that most of them were men. Hmm...)

Don't even think about completely avoiding the Chatter Devil by the approach of, *"I just won't give people anything to talk about."* While that's likely a prudent (and more ethical) posture, it will not totally stop the Chatter Devil. You will still be a Jelly person. You will still be interesting and fair game for leisure-time conversations. People will still want to know your business. *Just get over yourself and learn to live with it.*

CHAPTER 4
Don't Believe the Lies

I S THERE ANY one thing more valuable, more desirable, and more wonderful than a perfect diamond? Writers (and advertisers) wax poetic about the sparkle, the brilliance, the made-for-eternity beauty of diamonds. Diamonds are often used as the symbol of the "best" of whatever is being compared. Nothing is as precious as a perfect diamond! When the Precious Devil bites you, you believe that you are either the world's most perfect diamond, or a worthless lump of compressed coal.

There are two distinct and opposing illnesses that develop from the bite of the Precious Devil:

1. **Leaders believe that they are not and never will be as good as the others (just about any others) around them.**

   (I'm not just referring to emerging leaders with this statement. Matured leaders are not immune to the Precious Devil bite.) When the Devil bites, everyone else is more precious than they are. They are not perfect diamonds. They are flawed and unworthy. Why do they even have the temerity to consider leading others? They should be digging in the dirt with the chickens. They're only going to mess things up. They are not precious.

This unworthiness illness is not only potentially fatal to the leader—there is often collateral damage as well. This bite sometimes makes us turn on our own kind. While we are going down, we take other women with us.

2. **Leaders begin to believe that they are the most perfect of the diamonds.**
   They are the smartest, most valuable, strongest, most desirable "commodity" walking. They consistently make the right decisions, and whatever they choose to do is not only okay, it's close to brilliant. The rules and standards set by these bitten leaders must be adhered to without question. These brilliant leaders know what is best for every situation and for everyone. They are way too precious.

If left untreated, the bite of the Precious Devil is fatal to leaders, regardless of which way the illness appears—dirt-scratching worthless, or all-knowing, super-wonderful and diamond-perfect. Let's look the Precious Devil in the eye!

Digging in the Dirt With the Chickens

Dirt scratching sounds like this:

► *Why did Diane get that promotion instead of me? (If I had her connections, I wouldn't have to work 70 hours a week... for a lot less pay than she's getting!)*

▶ *Why does Jessica have it all when I have nothing? (If I had her money, I'd never work again! I'm not that good at it anyway.)*

▶ *Why can't I be as confident as Karen? (What do I have to be confident about? I'll walk in there and say, "I can do that," and I probably can't!)*

▶ *Why can't I do what Michele does? (Yeah, well she does **everything** right—besides she's smart and beautiful and everybody wants to be around her. I'm sick of hearing about precious Michele!)*

Have you ever said anything like one (or all) of these statements to yourself? You can admit it...no one else is listening. (I know that you don't usually say these things out loud. I sure don't! We know that we're not supposed to think this way. But then again, we do lots of things that we're not supposed to.) When we're busy measuring ourselves against others (and coming up on the short end of the comparisons), we sometimes throw in:

▶ *Why did that pimple have to show up today? It looks like a walnut stuck on my face! I've got nothing going for me!*

▶ *I have nothing to wear! Everything I own shows just how fat I really am! He's lying to me again—I **do** look fat in these pants!*

If someone else was attacking us the way we beat on ourselves— we'd be calling 911! Once we start dirt-scratching, it's all bad. This *"I'm not as good as... (fill in the blank)"* attitude is dangerous. There's this phenomenon of self-fulfilling prophesy that can come to pass. *"You think, therefore you are."* Or in this case, *"You think that you are not, therefore you are not."* Believe that you are unworthy long enough and you will be. This thinking is not good for you as a person, as a woman, or as a leader. You need to knock it off!

If you are thinking, *"Sure, easy for you to say—you've probably never felt that way,"* that would be wrong—I have done my time digging in the dirt with the chickens, and I'll probably do it again more than a few times in the future. We'll all go to the dirt-scratching place—we just need to know how to get out of there. The first step to raising ourselves above the dirt is to recognize that we have been lying in it for too long a time and accept that we need to take some conscious and definitive action to get out of there. If you wake up beating on yourself the way you did the day before, then it's time to stop. One bad day is okay. (Actually sometimes it's therapeutic if we're swinging too far the other way and believe that we are just too wonderful to associate with anyone else in the world. One day of breast-beating unworthiness can help level-set our own perception.) But two days in a row of digging in the dirt with the chickens? Now it's getting scary. If you keep that position long enough, it's suicidal. You will be right—you will be unworthy, undesirable, not valuable—you will have killed yourself as a leader.

Besides your own leadership death, you may also kill, or at the least maim, a few other worthy people along the way. When a woman has been attacked by the Precious Devil, she will either flee or fight. If she flees—then it's "only" suicide. If she fights, the collateral damage occurs because she often does not fight the Devil—she fights other powerful women around her. A bitten woman will sometimes seek to elevate her own self-perception by tearing down someone else's. When we feel strong, powerful, and confident, we take pleasure and pride in other women who are the same way. We seek their company and their counsel. But when we are insecure about our own abilities, there is a less-than-savory tendency to be resentful of, challenge, or do harm to another woman that may be perceived as "better, smarter, more valuable…" Some damaged, bitten leaders do not go "quietly into the night." They take others with them.

You will either recognize that you've been bitten by the Precious Devil because you've felt too low for too long or because others will tell you. If people close to you ask what's wrong more than once—then something must be wrong, and you'll want to thank them for pointing out that you need to pay attention...to you. After recognition of the situation, the next step in crippling the Precious Devil is to prepare your state of mind for the journey back to "I'm not only okay, I'm a valuable, talented woman and leader." You need some joy—any joy.

I first recognized the power of small doses of joy as the antidote to the unworthiness bite of the Precious Devil when I rose from my own dirt-scratching to shop for some peaches.

Life Lesson #5: Too Many Choices!

I was having a really bad week. I had been fighting with every-one at work, no one was listening to my ideas, I was stuck on the project I was working on, my kids were in trouble at school again, and I was retaining water like a new sponge. Because I don't dig with the chickens quietly, I was lashing out at all those who were offending me and just about anyone else who was in my line of sight. While I was punishing others, I was also telling myself, *"You've done this to your own self. Why can't you just shut up and get along? You are sooo stupid sometimes!"* Adding to my misery, I had company coming for dinner. Great! Now I have to produce something wonderful and engage in sparkling conversation with people I do not want to talk to. Okay, fine—I'll try my new recipe for peach cobbler, and if it doesn't turn out well, I can blame it on Betty Crocker.

Who knew there were so many kinds of peaches? Certainly not me. Great, something else I can't do right—I can't even select the right fruit! I asked the produce guy who was watering the rad-ishes if he knew about peaches. Oh yes—he definitely knew his peaches! He explained the difference between Lorings and Red Havens. He extolled the virtues of White Ladies and Jim Dandees. He explained why I didn't want to use the Red Rose or Summer Pearls for my cobbler and pointed me toward the Jersey Queens. The produce guy was so enthusiastic and joyful about those peaches that suddenly, I was too!

Peaches in hand (twice the number I needed actually), I walked in the door at home excitedly explaining just how wonderful that Jersey Queen peach was. I assembled my whole family so that they could share in my delight of having found the perfect fruit! All things were again right in my life.

My daughter was uncharacteristically quiet while I was holding the peach and twirling it a little to catch the best light on its perfect, peach-furry little body. She finally said, *"Mother, you do know that it's not the Hope Diamond, right? I mean, I'm glad that you're happier—finally—but it's only a peach."* I stopped the peach-spinning but continued smiling, because I knew this was an "epiphany" event.

No, it wasn't only a peach—it was a Life Lesson. *Get out of the dirt of unworthiness and misery by finding joy in something else.* The produce guy and the peach had pulled me right up out of the dirt and brought me back to joyful!

Reach for the Joy!

Maybe peaches don't do much for you. They may not, but there is something out there that will bring you joy when you feel that the rest of the world has turned against you...and that you are no longer a valuable person. Think about how you've overcome the Precious Devil bite of unworthiness in the past. Others may try to convince you that you're okay—probably better than okay—but you won't be ready for the messages from them (or from yourself) if you aren't in the right frame of mind. You need to be more joyful first. You need to identify and internalize some excitement about...something as the jump-start to re-building your excitement and confidence in yourself. You need to build a little passion about...anything because it can help carry you through to where you belong, which is the place of confidence that you are a valuable woman and leader.

You've reached for the joy in the past, but maybe instinctively and unconsciously. It's possible that you didn't realize what was happening. (I didn't fully understand the implications of the Choices lesson myself until I brought the peaches home—although I'm certain that other things had brought me joy and helped me get out of my funk in the past.) The Life Lesson of *"clean off the dirt of unworthiness and misery by finding joy in something else"* also includes *"and do it consciously and as quickly as you can!"* Although serendipitous joy is good, it can't be counted on to appear when you need it. The longer you stay in the dirt with the chickens, the more difficult it is to raise yourself out of it. Sometimes, you may need a reminder about what you need to do to avoid languishing in the unworthiness misery too long. Because I immediately shared my epiphany and the Life Lesson with my husband and daughter, I was able to create a Reminder Team for myself. I've heard several times over the years from each of them, *"You're really beating yourself up. Why don't you go and buy some peaches?"*

It has never again been peaches that have helped me help myself, but I've always managed to find something else. The buy-some-peaches suggestion reminds me to find my joy *du jour*—playing with my little dog Patches, or shopping online at Zappos for new shoes (whether or not I buy them), or making the world's best blueberry muffins and then promptly eating three of them. (See the Appendix for this recipe and for the peach cobbler, which turned out to be wonderful. I like to share good things—and these two treats are sinfully good!)

I recently received a wonderful gift of insight from a four-year-old girl and feel the need to share it with you. She showed me a powerful and eloquent demonstration of finding and using a small joy to feel good about myself and to build (or re-build) confidence.

An adorable, four-year-old girl was skipping into the store with her mother wearing a t-shirt and blue jeans—with a wide, pink net tutu over her jeans. She gave self-assured smiles to everyone she passed and reached out to wave to a little boy who was obviously enthralled with her. She looked wonderful, and she knew it! That child definitely had it goin' on!

Smiling at the delightful little girl, I said, "Blue Jean Ballerina," to her mother. Her resigned and slightly weary reply was, "Every day and everywhere." That little girl knew what made her joyful: a ballerina tutu even over her blue jeans. Maybe that doesn't work for you and me, but it sure worked for her. There is something out there that is your tutu or your peaches. Consciously reach out for those joyful things when the Precious Devil has bitten you. Get back to the mental and emotional place where you belong—where you have the excitement, energy, and confidence to be the fairest of them all.

When you are in the right (that is, more joyful) frame of mind, you'll be ready to look at the truth about yourself. If you feel the need to ask others to help re-build your knowledge about your value, then by all means do so. But don't believe that it will actually repair any ego damage that may have occurred during your "down" time. The truth about you will come only from you. It will come from objectively looking at what you've accomplished and what you plan to achieve. It will come from thinking about the people you helped along the way, as well as those who depend on you for your wisdom, guidance, and leadership. They depend on you because they trust that you can and will provide it for them. Look at the outward expressions of your value—the welcoming smiles of your colleagues as you join a meeting, the last e-mail or card you got that said, "Thanks", and the memo about the successful project you lead. Then revel in what you've done and how you are. You're good—know it!

However...don't take this knowledge too far. It could be the "other" bite of the Precious Devil.

All-Knowing, All-Powerful, and Impending Sainthood

The other illness that the bite of the Precious Devil can bring on is on the other side of the unworthiness spectrum. It's when leaders begin to believe that they are the most perfect of the diamonds. They are the smartest, most valuable, strongest, most desirable "commodity" walking. They consistently make the right decisions, and whatever they choose to do is not only okay, it's close to brilliant. The rules and standards set by these bitten leaders must be adhered to without question. These leaders know what is best for every situation and for everyone. They are way too precious!

Sometimes the illness presents itself this way.

Life Lesson #6: The Manners Maven

Mealtimes have been special, significant events for all of my adult life. They are much more than eating to sustain life. They are social events, discussion venues, and, while raising my children, opportunities for them to practice and perfect my lofty standards of perfect table manners. Meals, particularly dinner, carry a rigid and slightly pretentious set of rules:

▸ Food must never be placed on a bare table. A table cloth or placemats must be used for every meal, even if the "meal" consists of a peanut butter sandwich.

▸ The use of paper plates or napkins is a sign of America's moral decay. Only china dinnerware and cloth napkins are to be used.

▸ Meal attendees must be clean (not just hands) and fully clothed (including shoes) with combed hair.

▸ Conversation should be enlightening, informative, or thought-provoking, but must certainly be "appropriate to the dinner table."

▸ Proper table manners are to be employed at all times!

During one memorable dinner, my two daughters (ages 10 and 7 at the time) began to violate the mandate of proper table manners. They were suddenly and inexplicably doing horrible, ugly things. They were buttering an entire slice of bread at one time. They then moved on to placing a used fork directly on the tablecloth. And then the worst happened—they were talking with their mouths full!

After carefully placing my utensils at an angle on my plate and swallowing what I was eating, I began to lecture. Actually berate, harangue, and deliver a tirade would be more truthful. I talked and talked and talked about the importance of proper manners and why the girls should do as I've taught them, and how they would end up setting pins at a bowling alley if they never learned proper table etiquette. I harangued until their eyes glazed and their listening was long over. I talked until I couldn't stand the sound of my own voice! But I just could not stop myself! My mouth was spewing platitudes, but my brain was saying, "*What are you doing? Who made YOU the absolute authority of all things right? These kids will never listen to you again! You'd better recover from this! Just shut up!*" My final statement was,

"I hope that this lecture is not required again. I expect that you will remember what you've been taught and will behave appropriately at the table from now on." I then reached for my mashed potatoes, scooped up a big handful, and began to eat right out of my hand. Looks of complete shock immediately preceded my daughters' laughing so hard that they fell out of their chairs to the floor! "I guess I overdid that talk just a little," I suggested. Laughing and scrambling back into their chairs, they could only nod in agreement.

The Life Lesson that I taught myself was: You are never so right or so powerful that you can or should use any means available to make others "fall into line." If you can't appropriately lead others into the line, then maybe the line wasn't valid in the first place. Know the cost of using commando tactics—you may lose more than you gain.

Don't Believe all Your Own Press

Almost twenty years later, my oldest daughter was telling me about an incident at her office when she had to reverse an overbearing, inappropriately tough stand she had taken with an employee. She said, "I had to eat mashed potatoes with my hands." My daughter's table manners are still not up to my rigid standards, but she is a superior leader, and she will not be fatally bitten by the Precious Devil. She got the message—sometimes we're just not as smart, perfect, or precious as we think we are.

The Manners Maven Lesson demonstrated to me that I had been bitten by the Precious Devil. I was so right and so powerful that any means I wanted to use to make others "fall into line" was okay. I may have known the message, but I sure didn't know how to get it across effectively! My ego was blocking the transmission.

Sometimes ego can get in the way of your delivering superior leadership skills. Without being watchful for the Precious Devil, you can become a legend in your own mind. This does not negate the need for leaders to be confident. Leaders need appropriate, earned, honest confidence. The problem is that the Precious Devil can turn confidence into bravado or being dictatorial just because you can. Because others ask you so often for answers and guidance, and because you are often right with your responses, you might begin to believe that you are omniscient. You may expect that others are (or should be) gathering outside your door just to hear your sage counsel and to follow your lead. Whatever you do is okay. You can be heavy-handed or authoritarian. You don't have to ask for the input or agreement of others. You are not only a leader—you are the best leader that has ever lived, and it's unfortunate that the rest of the world just doesn't recognize that yet!

That you are the best leader that has ever lived is likely not true. The venom of the Precious Devil is probably coursing through your body. If you believe what the devil tells you and act on it, you may not be a leader for very long because you won't have many followers. And, even worse, you may quit trying hard to be a great leader. Why bother working at it? You've already made it! You're already a diamond—or even better, you could be a diamond-studded Rolex.

Part of the insidious nature of the Precious Devil is that it's so sneaky. It creeps in on the backs of awards and trophies, with raises and promotions, and on the laudatory comments of others. It can make you believe that all the praise is true. You believe your own press. You are the best there is.

How often have you talked to someone from a different city who is extolling the wonderfulness of their locale by saying that,

"Dr. Local Eyecare is the best ophthalmologist in the country," or, "Our high school is the best in the state," or, "This is the best pizza you will ever eat"? Can this be true? Does the best ophthalmologist in the country really practice in a town of 10,000 people in the north woods of Minnesota? If town residents believe that, it's okay. But if Dr. Eyecare, or the high school superintendent, or the pizza maker believes that, they may quit trying to be the best.

Malcolm Forbes shared the truth about diamonds and being the best when he said, "*Diamonds are nothing more than chunks of coal that stuck to their jobs.*" Leaders are the best when they just stick to their jobs. They don't believe that they've "made it" yet. They just keep trying.

Another reason why the Precious Devil is dangerous is that when he bites you, it just feels so good! It's natural to want to feel like the best all the time and to believe that we've "made it." It sure beats agonizing over our own worth or being afraid of making a decision because we don't trust our own abilities. That's the other side of the continuum. The best place for you and for your followers is somewhere to the right of the middle.

1_____5___(Here)_____10

I'm lower than dirt   I'm the most Precious in the Land

There are some proven ways to avoid the fatal bite of the Precious Devil. You don't need to ruminate on your faults, but someone needs to know and accept the reality of the adulation that you'll receive as a superior leader. That someone should be you. Were you really the most significant factor in your company's (or team's) success? Are you really the perfect role model for all those who follow you? Do you really possess "stellar leadership skills that will inspire generations of leaders to come"? Maybe you do. But possibly, you have to recognize that you weren't perfect; you could have done things just a little bit better. Don't beat yourself up—just be real and objective. You want to face realities and stick to your job of continuing to develop as, and be, a leader.

Be a Chameleon

Know and accept when you need to change "how you are" to accommodate the leadership needs of varying situations. Be willing to believe that you cannot be a "one size fits all" leader. Sometimes, despite the well-developed and proven skills you possess, you need to be and act differently. The skills and techniques required for strong leadership in one environment may not be the same in another. It doesn't matter if you know what needs to be accomplished; you must also get the message across in different environments and to people with different orientations. You may get comfortable with one style or approach and forget that it doesn't always translate well to other environments. You want to match your approach to the situation, the people, and the environment with which you are working.

> My boss, Paul Robson[1], is a superior leader and, more importantly for this anecdote, possesses exceptionally good taste in clothing, food, and décor. He once built a very large and beautiful "mansion" in Colorado that looked very Colorado-rustic—refined, elegant, woodsy, spendy. He decorated his massive, stone fireplace with deer antlers.
>
> ---
>
> [1] Paul Robson is the Vice President of the Lawson Practice of CIBER, Inc., a global information systems company. He has provided strong leadership to his organization for almost twenty years but may still have just a little more to learn about home decorating.

They were not just any deer antlers, however; they were huge, antique deer antlers! When Paul moved to a sophisticated, urban, downtown Chicago condominium, he brought the antlers and put them above the fireplace. What worked so well in Colorado definitely looked strange with the skyline of the Sears Tower in the background! Paul likely brought the antlers along because they were so perfect in Denver and because they were so expensive! My job as Strategist with our company includes providing strategic consulting to Paul. I stretch that role to include decorating advice and once pointed out that the antlers just didn't make it in the Chicago environment. Paul then countered with, *"But they cost a bundle!"* I suggested, *"Donate them to some worthy charity and take the tax-deduction."*

The image of those "out-of-environment" antlers comes to mind whenever I see the need for myself or others to change because the situation and/or the people have changed. While talking to my husband (who serves as my 24/7 sounding board) about why an approach I'm using is not working, I have said more than once, *"I need to take down the antlers."* If your leadership is not making a positive impact, it may be time for you to donate those antlers.

An example that's closer to the "business" of leading is a client that I worked with on the West Coast. (This client needs to remain nameless.) For this client, I was to provide strategic consulting to ensure that their newly-developed business processes matched their business model. They were an extremely challenging organization to do business with. They were argumentative to the point of combative and direct almost to being abusive, and they just would not listen to the advice from me that they were paying for. Then I discovered that the all-male executive staff came from a police background. They treated each other and their business partners like they were all "perps"! The problem was not a gender issue, which I had first suspected. The executives responded well to other women in their organization, as long as those women were also "in their faces." Having seen every episode of every variation of the *Law and Order* series on TV, I knew how to act. In the environment of perp versus cop, I needed to be a cop, not a perp! Changing my approach turned a losing battle into a collaborative, successful engagement. We all won.

Sometimes, you have to know when your tried and true skills are not applicable. It may be time to be a chameleon and develop or practice new or different skills and approaches. Don't believe that you are automatically the best that can be in all situations.

Don't Take Yourself Too Seriously

Sometimes we all do things that are just dumb. When this happens, it's much better to laugh at ourselves, because certainly others will be laughing. It's not wonderful to hear, *"I'm not laughing **at** you, I'm laughing **with** you,"* if you are not laughing! If the Precious Devil has bitten you and you really believe that whatever you do is the right thing to do, there will be many times when people are, in fact, laughing at you and not with you.

> Many years ago, my husband and I took three of our children to Disneyland. We'd been there several times and knew the territory, so we didn't feel any particular need to pay close attention to where we parked. We were too excited to begin the adventure to bother with details. We just led our eager group on to see the Mouse! Fourteen hours later, we were totally Moused-out and really wanted to go home. We quickly realized that we had a problem, however. The parking lot had filled during the day, and we now had no idea where our car was in the midst of the 10,000 others.

> Because we thought we knew the territory and neglected to account for changes in the scenery (from the other cars to-ing and fro-ing), we had no choice but to stand around for another two hours and wait until all 10,000 other cars left! Only then could we find our car, which was safely parked in the Bambi section. For the next twenty years, *"You parked in Bambi,"* has been our family's cue to indicate, *"You've really done something dumb, and you may as well start laughing, because I'm going to!"*

Not taking yourself too seriously, realizing when you've made a mistake and shaking it off, is appropriately humbling. It will keep you from being totally eaten by the Precious Devil. Your leadership will live long, and everyone will prosper—you and your followers!

CHAPTER 5
Don't Get Buried

ALL TRUE LEADERS are at least a little obsessive-compulsive. What else accounts for the 24/7 quest to excel, to continue to improve and develop, to lead others—even when it is seriously challenging to do so? What drives leaders too early from their warm beds, or birthday parties, or vacations to finish a leadership task? What compels them to put themselves at personal risk of failure time and again by stepping up to a leadership role? Answer is: They are obsessive-compulsive.

I'm not using the clinical definition of OCD: A psychiatric anxiety disorder most commonly characterized by a subject's obsessive, distressing, intrusive thoughts and related compulsions (tasks or "rituals") that attempt to neutralize the obsessions.

The colloquial definition of OCD more aptly applies to leaders: A descriptor for someone who is excessively absorbed in or fixated on a cause or pattern of behavior and who is often meticulous to the point of requiring perfectionism. In the context of leadership, a person does not **have** OCD, they **are** OCD.

I remember vividly the first time that someone pointed out to me that my "OCD was showing." I was irritated, insulted, and totally disbelieving. I was not OCD. I only wanted things to be done properly! And I wanted them now! I displayed only a little of my angst to my "accuser," but then stomped off to think about the statement. I followed my usual thought-processing model and made a list of all the OCD behaviors that I could think of. I then listed the reasons why I was **not** obsessive-compulsive next to the behaviors. In order to examine them more easily, I then thought about whether or not I should priority rank the behaviors or list them alphabetically. The harsh light bulb of reality went on. My accuser was right. I was being OCD just to prove that I was not! Okay, I thought; I will accept this, and I will work it to my advantage!

You will be well served if you also accept that much of what drives you to leadership excellence is that you are likely at least a little OCD. There's probably research about this, but I don't feel the need to search for it. I already believe it's likely that most women are at least a little OCD. The majority of the women I've ever known play so many concurrent roles that if they were not absorbed and fixated on getting them all done—they wouldn't happen. Wage-earner, wife, cook, mother, chauffeur, counselor, lover, decorator, judge, organizer—the list could continue for pages! You know this—you live it. How would you get it all done if you weren't at least a little "absorbed and fixated"? Are we "often meticulous to the point of requiring perfection"? Well, sure we are! If we don't stand there scrubbing at that stain on his new shirt, who will? If we don't pay attention to all the details (of everything), will they be tended to or just overlooked and snarl up something else down the road? We live in a state of OCD for survival, and in most cases, all those others around us benefit from our compulsive behavior.

All of the counsel that's coming up in *Pink Leadership* and the suggestions for keeping the OCD Devil in check are written from the perspective of your leadership role. I'm not venturing into the territory of redefining or advising you about your OCD-ness at home. You're probably not going to stop being compulsive and working too hard and too long in your personal, family life. You are a woman...that's what you do...and that's probably what you need to do to keep everyone at your house upright, clothed, clean, well-behaved (children and spouses are included in this), fed, and on time for appointments. But at the least, you can work on reining in the OCD Devil at work.

Determine that OCD-ness is a good thing. Make it work for you! However, pick your focus, your time, and your intensity. Don't just ignore that you are the way you are, because the OCD Devil will sneak up while you're distracted doing everything that you do. He will bury your leadership with his you-have-to-do-everything-right-now-and-perfect lists.

The OCD Devil will mutate perfectly appropriate leadership behaviors and make you:

- ► Lose sight of the bigger picture while you are focusing on having everything just right
- ► Believe that it's okay to want everything and want it now
- ► Work so hard and so long that you will burn out before your task as a leader is done

The OCD Devil is setting you up for some kind of ugly after-life OCD hell. When leaders go to OCD hell, they find out that there is no one there to lead. There are no followers! There is nothing to do, and they can't even remodel or clean their solitary rooms! For OCD people, this scenario is agony for eternity.

There are some ways to avoid the OCD Devil.

Identify the OCD Devil's Moves

You may as well leverage your OCD tendency to define, and probably list…everything. Work it!

Seek good counsel from another leader—someone you trust and who will tell you the truth about your list. Are you evidencing good leadership or are you just being OCD? Listen to what your "counselor" tells you without being defensive. (Definitely don't "kill the messenger." You may need that messenger's help again in the future!) Then, modify your behavior, attitude, or focus to get out of excessive OCD behavior and into good leadership posture. Another word for "messenger" in this context would be mentor. Your best mentor (or multiple mentors) will provide good counsel and will not be afraid to confront a strong leader (you!) with ugliness when it's required. Find the truth-teller in your list of mentors, seek that person's counsel, and listen. You do not have all the answers about and for yourself. We often have to follow Blanche Dubois' lead and depend "on the kindness of strangers" (read: mentors).

It's amazing how many leaders really do want everything now and have a difficult time understanding why they can't have it. They are defining the goals well; they are leading/guiding/counseling/managing well. Why can't everyone else just fall into line? Why can't all the good planets align to give them all of exactly what they want, when and how they want it? This alignment doesn't always happen because the leader is not the only factor in the accomplishment equation. The biggest "other factor" is the group of people who will actually follow and act on leading/guiding/counseling/managing. Often, there are other limiters as well, such as politics or budgets, priority-shifts from others, or just not enough time.

A leader with whom I work (and who needs to remain nameless here) has said more than once to me, *"But, I want it **all** now!"* Despite this leadership aberration, the leader regularly displays superior leadership until he reaches for the unattainable—everything and now! That's when I know he's in the clutches of the OCD Devil and needs a serious jolt of reality.

> We recently entertained our niece, Tami Langsdorf, and her husband Dave at our home for brunch. I included on the menu one of my super-easy and seriously wonderful treats: Beer Bread Toast. (See the Appendix for the recipe.) The first batch of toast went so quickly that I hastened to make more. (I come from an Italian orientation to feeding others. You must always have an excess of food on the table. Allowing a guest to go hungry is the fast track to hell.) As I set the newly toasted Beer Bread on the table, Tami reached quickly for another piece. She then exclaimed, *"Look what I've done! I'm not even finished with my other toast and I'm already grabbing for more! Now I have a whole plate of nothing but bread!"* While we all laughed with her (yes, she was laughing at herself), the image of the "I-want-it-**all**-now" leader flashed in my head. That's what too often happens. We grab for all of it and end up with just a whole plate full of bread!

This I-want-it-all-and-I-want-it-now aspect of the OCD Devil can be killed, or at the least seriously wounded, by the magic word "Why?" Why do you want this? Why is this an endeavor that is worthy of your focus? Why do you think it is not happening? Why are other things or people getting in the way of success? Why should this be on the list of "want it and now"? Questioning your motivations, your personal drive, and the limitations of what is possible will allow you to prioritize and to target those worthy quests to what "should be." You may not have everything exactly when you want it and how you want it; however, you may have what is possible and what you should have.

Watch Out for Burnout

Learn to pace and discipline yourself, and re-learn and re-tool the pacing and the self-discipline often. Build your own motivation to go forward, and create and use your own recovery systems.

Burnout is the worst of the OCD Devil attacks, and it can be fatal to a leader. You can no longer provide leadership to others if you cannot keep up the pace. No one ever won a marathon by sitting down at the eleventh mile marker.

There are a few twists to this aspect of the OCD Devil:

▶ Working too hard and too long when it's not justified or required: burning the midnight oil

▶ Not setting the pace for the long haul: sprinting for 26 miles

▶ Not seeking and using recovery systems: not rising from the ashes

Burning the Midnight Oil

What can you do if you have a tendency to work too hard or too long? (The question is written as though you may *not* have this tendency. I'm just being polite. If you are a leader, you often do work too hard and too long!) The first remedy is to recognize the problem. Listen to those who are in a position to know the difference between good, old-fashioned hard work, and over-the-top effort. You may not want to listen to someone who knows what's happening in several soap operas or whose idea of hard work is to primarily just "think about what they need to get done." However, you should listen, without being defensive, to someone who is also a hard worker and who is in a position to observe what you are doing to yourself. If that person says, *"You're hurting yourself,"* then stop doing that! You are likely hurting others, too. You may have a right to hurt yourself, but you certainly don't have the right to inflict the effects of your OCD Devil on others.

There are some people who believe that "pulling an all-nighter" is needed quite often. This behavior is a throwback to their college days, when they spent most of their time before Final Exams being distracted by collegiate-life "recreational opportunities" (read: partying, drinking, dancing, and often more intimate socializing). At some point, usually at 10:00 p.m. the night before the test, it occurred to them that they may need to study. They carry forward this habit into their work lives and may even brag about often doing all-nighters. These people are not real leaders. They obviously can't prioritize, are not sufficiently disciplined to stay on target to the task, and are not leading in a direction that others will want to follow. If you often have to pull all-nighters, you may want to re-think your desire and ability to be a leader. You have a challenge to work out of yourself. You can still become a high-quality, valued leader. You just need to focus on killing the all-nighter approach. Get ahead of the work. Place your priorities where they should be.

Sometimes brief spurts of excessive effort or time are really required. Examples are when you're kicking off or completing a new initiative or when a project is dangerously stalled. But occasionally, time and energy are expended just because you can. Writers are often asked why they write. My favorite response (from a forgotten author) is that, *"I write because I have to."* Some leaders lead whatever they see or dream up just because they have to—they are compelled to lead. One of the characteristics of an OCD leader is that, when faced without a challenge, the leader will make one (or more). The OCD leader will then add those additional challenges to the growing list of "have-to-dos" until they are buried and burned by the midnight oil.

Stab that OCD Devil in his evil heart. Ask the "Why" questions? Why am I doing this? Why do I think I need to devote this much time and effort? Why can't I stop?

Sprinting for 26 Miles

How can you pace yourself properly? Many leaders only have one speed—as fast and as hard as they can go.

> Why do they call marathons, marathons? It seems that in 490 BC, there was a fierce and important battle between the Greeks and the Persians near a city called Marathon. After the Greeks won the fight, a messenger ran to Athens, which was approximately 26 miles from Marathon. He entered the city square and shouted, "Nike!" which is Greek for victory. He then fell to the ground, dead from the exertion of the full-out-speed, 26-mile run. It is not a good thing to run like the Marathon messenger. He certainly never got a chance to deliver another important message.

Setting your own right pace is difficult. Going at your tasks at Nike speed just creeps up on you. One minute you're working at the right pace for the right amount of time. You suddenly look around and realize that you haven't stopped and you are exhausted, and frankly, most of what you've done in the last few hours, days, or weeks is not too good! Nothing else may happen (that needs to) while you are full out, totally focused at the wrong pace.

> For a number of reasons, both personal and professional, I recently re-negotiated my professional role with my boss to reduce the work hours required of me to no more than 40 hours per week, unless there was some compelling need for more of my time. To a compulsive over-achiever with the OCD Devil always perched on my shoulder, that's like working part-time. I knew that I would have a difficult time adjusting to my new schedule, so I asked to start the new schedule two months after the agreement was reached. I needed time to practice not working all the time! This is a sad commentary on my own compulsion. I justify sharing this because it's important to know our own limitations. Sometimes you may have to trick yourself or even practice working at the right pace. If that's what it takes to get the pace right, then it's a good thing to do.

I often trick myself or create "rules" that I have to follow to pace myself properly. I recently discovered a Web site (www.freerice.com) that allows you to earn rice that will be donated through the UN World Food Program to help end hunger. You earn 20 grains of rice for every word that you can define correctly. Pick the right multiple-choice response, and you will see 20 grains of rice appear in the bowl. This activity is right up my alley! I love knowing words and learning new ones. (I was the nerd in school who carried a notebook to write down every new word I heard every day. My "friends" made fun of me. I didn't care.) I do care about stopping world hunger, and here's a way that I can help without leaving my computer, or even sending money! On my first visit to the site, I was unable to stop myself. I just kept hitting the button, hitting the button, defining the words again and again, seeing the rice bowl fill up. The problem was that's all I was doing for a very long time. So, I had to make a rule for myself. Every morning, freerice.com is my first Web site of the day. I define the words until I miss one. Then I do one more. (I do hate to stop as a "loser.") Then I'm done with the site until the next day. This is an example of a pacing rule. You likely can think up your own tricks and rules. Sometimes, that's what you'll need to do. If pacing won't come naturally, trick yourself and believe the trick, or make rules...and follow them!

Don't shout, "Nike!" and then fall to the ground. Be watchful and listen to others (credible, hard-working, caring others) who raise the flag when your pace is too furious. Ask, "Why?" Why do I have to do this right now? Why can't I stop? Listen to your own answers. Slow it down. Spread out the activities a little more. You will likely do a better job, and you will not be wounded by the OCD Devil. (I'm not going to offer the platitude of "stop to smell the roses." I know what happens when you do slow down long enough for that. You prune the bush, or re-arrange the cut flowers in a new vase, or decide that you need to re-paint your bedroom to match the apricot color of that Antigua Rose. I know how you are.)

Rise From the Ashes!

Do you believe that burnout is for wimps? Do you believe that you are the Energizer Bunny that will keep going and going long after the others have fallen grasping for their computers and spreadsheets? If you do, then you are either:

► Still early in your formative leadership development and have not yet "hit the wall," so you're not exactly sure what that means

► Right now in the darkness of massive burnout and in denial about it

► Relying heavily on the "miracles of modern pharmacology" to survive

The leader is the heartbeat of the team, department, division, or company. If your heart is no longer able to beat in the rhythm that's required to sustain quality leadership, the rest of the people will also experience serious "palpitations" and be unable to function effectively.

Leadership burnout is closely related to the pacing element of the OCD Devil. It's what happens when the devil has delivered his fatal blows and has made you run too hard for too long. You may no longer have the desire, the mental stamina, or the physical energy to deal with yet another problem, one more resistant follower, or any other roadblocks to your success. You are **done**! You are burned out. You are unable to lead effectively. You likely can't even follow well.

When you, as a leader, burn out, the impact is more far-reaching than for a "regular" person's burnout. When the leader is no longer willing and able to lead well, nothing too positive happens. The leader's followers will become confused, de-motivated, or even alienated from the leader. The objectives of whatever it is you were leading toward become cloudy, or change, and may not ever be reached.

In my book, *Be the Horse or the Jockey: 110 Tips and Techniques for Followers...and Leaders*, I wrote about burnout. Just in case you missed it in *Horse or Jockey* and since I don't believe I can improve on what I already wrote—I'm offering it again here for you.

If you are not sure you are approaching burnout because you haven't experienced it before or don't realize that you have, you may not recognize the symptoms. If you are currently burned out but may be trying to delude yourself, you should also pay close attention to the signs of danger. (If you are trying to deal with potential burnout with a "better living through chemistry" approach—just stop that craziness! Drugs and alcohol won't fix the situation and will eventually destroy your leadership. Besides, they're expensive.)

What are the symptoms of leadership burnout? How do you know that you've been hit between the eyes by the OCD Devil? The following are some of the signs that you are burning out as a leader. Have you or are you experiencing any of these?

► If someone says, *"I have a question for you,"* do you immediately think, *"And I have an answer and that is for you to SHUT UP"*?

► Do you often lie awake at night thinking about what you have to accomplish next, but you can't come up with the solution? (Nighttime analysis is often a positive technique if it regularly results in some kind of answer or at the least, a feeling of peace because you have addressed the issues. If there is no answer or no peace, then you are not analyzing, you are burning.)

► Are you tired of people saying, *"You look tired; are you all right?"* when you didn't know you looked tired? When they ask that, do you suspect that they are just jealous and/or trying to undermine you?

► Do you now look at a delay, a budget cutback, or a team member loss as a problem, when previously it would have been just a challenge to overcome? Does everything suddenly seem harder?

► Are you deciding that input from others and patience are highly overrated and that others just need to do what you're telling them to do and quit with their incessant questioning?

► Do you "hate everybody"?

You may be burning out as a leader.

I was once trying to comfort my daughter Julie who was reacting to a difficult personal situation. I offered the time-tested platitude of, *"Just remember—that which does not kill you makes you stronger."* She gave me a jaded, sideways look and countered with, *"No, that which does not kill you simply weakens you for the next blow."* That stopped me in my advisory track! She was right! Just how many times can we take a hit? How many times can we face consecutive challenges well if we haven't regained our strength from the last ones? The X number of blows before you are destroyed is not a number to try to identify. Just figure it's there and seek to avoid getting close to it.

Life Lesson #7: Shake It Off!

My brother Jim began his long teaching career as a passionate, devoted, high school basketball coach. He was completely committed to the personal, academic, and team sports successes of his players. He was also an extraordinarily well-loved leader and an inordinately tough task master.

Jim had a philosophy that a player should not commit a foul without a reason. However, if you do foul another player, that player should not be able to get up right away. And more, if you were the one that had the foul counted against you, you'd better "shake it off" and immediately get back into the game.

Any time one of his players committed a foul, Jim's eyes were totally fixed on his offending player. He would begin to shout his mantra of, *"Shake it off! Get in the game! Shake it off!"* If he did not see immediate signs of recovery from his player, Jim would pull the player from the game and he would sit on the bench for a while and "recover."

During one game, one of Jim's players was charged with a two-point foul. Jim focused intently on his player and exhorted him (very loudly) to shake it off. As the play immediately continued, his player made several gestures of, "I didn't do it," and displayed anger at the referee and at the other team. Jim didn't just bench this player. He sent him to the locker room. He would no longer look at the player. He looked down, shook his head, and with his arm fully extended, pointed to the locker room. Jim kicked the player out of the game in front of everyone!

During our traditional, family post-game analysis later that night, I said that was such a terrible thing to do—punishing that player in front of everyone was excessive and embarrassing when the kid was just reacting normally. Jim turned on me with his usual ferocity and said, *"What are you thinking? That kid is the Team Captain! He **has** to come back fast or no one else will know they have to! I was not about to let him do that to himself or to my other kids. He can either stay in the game and do what he's supposed to, or he sits it out. He'll get over being kicked out. I'm not about to validate that it's okay to act like that. I won't let him lose the respect of the rest of the team. He has to show that he can take the hit and come back from it."* Jim concluded his lecture to me by saying, *"How about if you just stick to doing whatever it is you do and let me coach?"*

Jim was right. The Life Lesson here was that *we need to do whatever it takes to recover for both ourselves and for the others who we lead.*

Do What It Takes to Stay in the Game

Like all recovery programs, the first step is acknowledgement of the problem. You need to stand in front of the mirror (preferably alone and fully clothed...or not) and say, "*Hi. My name is Jennifer, and I am burning out as a leader.*" (This is not a statement to share with the masses. Knowledge of your potentially imminent death as their effective leader will help neither your followers nor your recovery.) Listen to yourself say this, and believe yourself. Why shouldn't you? Don't others believe you? Aren't you an excellent leader? Lead yourself into recovery!

Similar to the need to trick yourself or create rules to allow yourself to pace properly, you will want to identify, build in, and execute recovery mechanisms to prevent or stop the OCD Devil burnout. These tricks and rules are as unique as you are. There is no one-stop shop for preventing burnout. There are no To-Do lists that will apply to everyone. Knowing the tricks or rules that will work for you starts with knowing yourself. What makes you feel better about yourself and what you are doing and accomplishing? Recovery techniques are most often not complex or difficult to execute. If they are, then they may add even more burden to you. The most effective recoveries are often simple and short. They leverage the life lessons that you have learned about how you are and what you need.

I am sometimes amused (but always irritated) when others tell me, "*What you need to do is take a nice long vacation and just lie on the beach for a week.*" Maybe that's what they need to do, but not me! Chronic over-achiever that I am—just planning the vacation and getting my work done in advance, when I already feel overburdened, could put me right over the edge. Besides that trauma, the thought of being prone on hot, wet sand for a week raises my anxiety level. But a beach vacation might work for you. If you've come back from quiet getaways recharged and ready to jump back into the fray, then that's what you should do. This is not a recovery mechanism that will work often, however, unless you have a massive amount of accrued vacation time and unlimited funds to take you to that peaceful beach whenever you need to go. So what do you do in between those major recharging events?

The examples of my own recovery techniques are offered in the spirit of jump-starting your thinking about what you need. Not all, and possibly not one, will work for you, but maybe they'll help you realize what you need to do to recover. The first step in identifying and designing your own recovery system does apply to everyone, however. That step is to consciously recognize that what you are doing is healing yourself. You are building strength for the next blow. You not only have the right to do that, you have the obligation as a leader to ensure that you are strong, willing, and able to lead again.

After your acceptance of your own need to heal, then you might try some of my tricks.

> ▶ **Find a healing place to go to mentally.** I've long held on to an idealized (and I realize, completely unrealistic) vision of living on a farm. When life is too chaotic, and I recognize that I'm out-of-control and need to recover, I let my mind wander to my home on the farm.
>
> Fade in to the scene. I'm sitting in the shade on a green (well-manicured by someone else) lawn under an extravagant oak tree with my collie dog Lady. I'm reading quietly and Lady is keeping me company. (I think Lady is mute— she never barks.) I'm wearing a Gone with the Wind dress with a big bow in the back that is absolutely stunning! In the background is the main house, which must have aluminum siding since it never needs painting. There is a white picket fence all around the yard, which does need a fresh coat of paint periodically. (I need something to do on my farm besides read! Feeding the animals and cleaning out pig pens are not in my farm vision. I don't know who does that, but it's sure not me.) Sometimes Lady and I will walk down the long driveway together to

collect the mail. (There's not a lot of mail to carry back since I don't give out the address.) As we walk along, Lady stays right by my side, but her wagging tail never touches me. We are just there—together but separate, walking down the road. Fade out. Works for me!

I have an alternate place that I go to when the farm is just too peaceful, but I don't advertise that particular mental journey. One time when my husband saw me looking contemplative, he asked if I was at the farm. I said, *"No, I'm not ready for that much tranquility. I just need to escape. I'm going to my place under the bridge where the sex-crazed trolls live."* He was not thrilled with that recovery technique. (His reaction was a reminder that there are some thoughts that I just shouldn't share.)

► **Quietly celebrate your own victories.** I do not seek or need the praise of others to recover. (I certainly don't reject it, however! I like it, but it's not a have-to-have to heal.) I need my own praise. When I reach the end of a long, hard work road, I need to look at what I've accomplished and bask for a few minutes in its "wonderfulness." I clear off the dining room table (or the hotel desk) and place the physical evidence of the accomplishment in the middle. The evidence can be a document, a spreadsheet, a report, an e-mail of thanks from a team member or supervisor, a pay stub that shows a bonus, or the results from the fundraiser I led. There is something that says, *"I did it."* Then I just look at the piece of evidence and say to myself, *"That was good. It was ugly for a while, but now—look! It is successful, and I did it."* I will smile at myself smugly, mentally pat myself on the back, and then be ready to tackle the next challenge.

▶ **Rest often for brief periods whenever you can.** I am addicted to naps. I think about them when I'm not napping, I plan for them, I savor the opportunities. I can nap lying down, sitting, or standing, and will try to nap every day for 2 minutes to 30 minutes depending on the opportunity. (Naps in the middle of a conference call are usually pretty short!) I know that my best thinking times are early in the morning and in the early evening. I contend that anyone who pays me for work at 2:30 in the afternoon is not getting their money's worth. That's prime nap time! I may be physically present, and I may appear to be working, but if I'm expected to do anything too difficult, if I have to make too many important decisions at 2:30 p.m., they will be long in coming and not my best efforts. I try to avoid or not schedule the difficult meetings or conversations for that time. I don't start a new project or response to a challenge in the afternoon. If I'm forced by circumstance to do that too often, I know I'll be headed down the path to burnout because I have to push myself too hard to accomplish what should be easier for me.

▶ **Play with your dog (or your children).** When the rest of the world is trying to grind me to dust, my dog Patches will only require me to throw her stuffed kitty a few times to make her happy. And that makes me happy. Stepping away from the environment and the thought processes that are trying to overwhelm me is my quick reward and re-charger to allow me to jump back into the fray.

▶ **Get something finished and right.** When a project is going on too long and the demands are getting too great and the blows are coming too quickly, I just need to get something done that will please me and put a smile on someone else's face. That smile helps me forget or accept the frown-y faces of others who are causing my pain. When I need to get something finished quickly and right, I will either make a spectacular dinner or, if I'm short on time or ingredients, I'll make a non-healthy, special dessert. Because I'm OCD, I have a page in my recipe book with already-identified personal stress-relieving recipes. They are not too hard, don't take too long to make, and always result in applause. (See the Appendix for my top two choices: Pasta Carbonara [Sophia Loren's recipe], and Homemade Chocolate Pudding. Sure winners in my house!) When I'm done and warming myself in the glow of accomplishment and the overly-fed smiles of my family, I know that I'm okay. I may not yet have figured out how to get the rest of the company to accept my ideas for changing the methodology we use on clients' projects, but I can still make a mean chocolate pudding!

What works for you? What will allow you to recover in between the blows so that you aren't weakened to the point of leadership death? Figure out what those recovery techniques are and then rise from the ashes. Be ready, willing, and strong enough to continue leading!

The last four chapters of *Pink Leadership* have been about dodging, battling, or outsmarting the Leadership Devils. The focus so far has been on what to avoid. Now it's time to move past the "avoidance" and on to the "action."

CHAPTER 6
Do What Leaders Do!

WHAT **EXACTLY** DOES this mean—"Do what leaders do"? You may also be familiar with the variations of, *"If you're going to talk the talk, you've got to walk the walk,"* and, *"Talk the talk and walk the talk."* Whichever seems to make the most sense to you, they likely both mean, *"Act the way you say you're going to."* In the context of leadership, this statement translates to, *"Both say and do leadership 'things.'"*

Throughout your life, you may have heard the following exhortations, often from a parent, and generally in this order:

▸ *Act like a big kid.* (Sometimes accompanied by, *"Big girls don't cry."*)

▸ *Grow up. You're in the fifth grade—you're not a baby anymore.*

▸ *Don't even think that you're an adult yet. You're just a teenager, and you need to act your age.*

▸ *You're an adult. Start acting like one.* (You may have heard this one multiple times from various people.)

Have you ever asked the person saying these things to you just what a big girl or not-a-baby or a teenager or an adult actually acts like? (If you have asked and have received any good answers, please share them. I asked specifically several times about the standard, acceptable behavior when I was a teenager. If there was a good answer, I couldn't hear it through the loud hollering my question seemed to bring on. I'm still not sure of the answer.) But whether or not you've asked, have you wondered just what that means? If you weren't supposed to be doing...whatever it was that brought on those age-specific lectures, then how did you know exactly what it is that you **were** supposed to be doing? It never seemed to be as easy as "just do the opposite of what you're doing now." Clarity in communication should be taught in parenting classes!

When leaders are admonished to "walk the talk," just what does that walk look like? Is it a purposeful, on-target, solid stride while wearing sensible, low-heeled pumps? Or is it "motivating," exciting and fluid, balanced on too-high heels? Whether you are an emerging leader or a practiced, looking-to-perfect-your-skills leader, you may have questions about the specifics of those talking and walking points. However the walk looks, it seems to be mandated by the talking part. So, what words are leaders walking to?

Life Lesson #8: Just Like His Mother

Many years ago, during the heydays of the federal government "Poverty Programs" such as Head Start, Job Corps, and others, I was the Director of Family Planning for southeast Missouri. The mission of the Family Planning Program was to provide education about and clinical services for the medically indigent (read: below poverty-level), and the program was funded by grants from the U.S. Department of Health, Education, and Welfare (HEW).

During my tenure with the Family Planning Program, I was affectionately referred to by my clients as the "Rubber Lady." My mother was not delighted.

For about two years, the definition of clinical services was expanded by HEW to include pre-screening for referrals for psychological counseling in the area of sexual dysfunction. I was less than thrilled when I was informed that I would be trained and certified as a Sexual Therapy Counselor. I did not, however, intend to lose my government grant, so I prepared to be trained for and subsequently deliver on something for which I was woefully unqualified.

For reasons that were a mystery to me, the University of Nebraska was designated as the place where the training would occur. I could not figure out why Nebraska was selected as the hotbed of sexual dysfunction counseling, but it must have been, because that's where they sent me.

The training included many less-than-completely-comfortable, although very interesting, elements. One of these was "de-sensitization," which consisted primarily of viewing hard-core pornographic videos of every possible sexual combination and activity imaginable. (Many of the groupings and activities I had NOT imagined before I spent almost 40 hours watching porn. Most of the videos were produced with government funds, by the way. Your tax dollars at work! Amazing.) The objective of the de-sensitization was to make us "shock-proof" so that we could address any topic without surprise, alarm, or being personally judgmental. The first 20 hours of viewing (in a mixed-gender group) were...shocking! The next 20 hours were boring. The de-sensitization exercise seemed to have worked pretty well for me. (It was a long time before anyone or anything actually "appealed" to me again.)

Most of my anxiety during training actually centered on the **words** that I needed to counsel effectively. I almost pleaded with my instructors to answer, "*What am I supposed to say? What are the words when someone has just told me about their problems?*" Each time I asked, the answer was the same: "*When you truly understand the problem and the resolutions, you will know what words to use.*" Obviously I did not "truly understand" because I struggled horribly to think of the appropriate responses to the many role-playing scenarios we practiced. I just barely passed the training.

Two weeks after receiving my hard-earned certification, it was Clinic Day at our Family Planning Clinic. It was one of the once-a-week days when our volunteer physicians provided free gynecological exams to our clients. I looked through the front window of our Family Planning Clinic and saw a young man sitting on the steps with his head in his hands, obviously very distraught. I asked our front office medical assistant if she had talked to him. This was our conversation:

Assistant: "*I think he's crazy or something. He wanted a pap smear! He said his mother had died of ovarian cancer and he was really worried about getting it. I told him he didn't have the right 'stuff' for us to check in the exam room.*"

Jeanne: "*Does he meet our income guidelines for service?*"

Assistant: "*Oh, yeah. He's part of the* (name deleted) *family. We have lots of them here. But he didn't come in with them. I don't think they like him very much. You'll see why.*" I went outside to meet the young man and, as the assistant had predicted, I did see why the rest of the mountain-men in the family would not like him very much. (It was common for entire families to accompany their wives/sisters/daughters into town for Clinic Day, in groups as large as 20 people, so I had already met many of the men.)

The unhappy man on the steps of the clinic was in his middle twenties, slight of build, and reasonably attractive—although he was disheveled, and his personal hygiene was a little suspect, like the rest of his clan. When the young man looked up at me, I could tell that his tears had made his mascara run and his hair (although not too clean) still showed the "roller marks" from having his curlers in too tight. Although homosexuality was not unheard of in the Missouri hill families that we served, we had not come across any cross-dressing or transsexual tendencies before.

I asked the young man why he was so unhappy on such a nice fall day. In a rush of words, he explained that his mother had died and he missed her terribly and he was so afraid that he would get the same "disease." I told him that I knew his mother. That I had met her two months before and had arranged for some of the pain medicines that she needed at the end. (We had discovered his mother's health problem through a home visit made by one of our outreach workers. It was already much too late for her by then.) I asked him why he thought he would get his mother's problem since that was "woman trouble."

He said, *"Can't you see? I'm just like my mother! I've always been just like my mother! I was her baby and whatever she did, I did."* (He was the youngest of his mother's 13 children.) *"I want to be a good mother like she was, but I'll never be able to if I die from her disease."*

Suddenly, I knew the words because I understood the immediate problem in front of me. I saw a frightened, confused little boy (regardless of his age), who really did believe that he was just like his mother. He didn't believe that he **should** be a woman. He believed that he already was. The words that were needed were accepting, compassionate, "motherly" words.

It was not my task to "fix" the young man's gender-confusion. My role was to identify and deal with the immediate challenge.

I needed to provide acceptance first, and then support and comfort to build trust with him so that we could help him further. I told the young man that our nurse in the office probably sent him away because she thought we didn't have an open time for the doctor to see him. But, as luck would have it, I could get him seen right away. (I didn't want the young man hanging around the waiting room because I knew there would be a high potential for public ridicule by our other clients.) I told him that if I could get him tested right away, he needed to go to another doctor who would help him also. He agreed, so I walked him right to an open exam room and gave him instructions on how to get his feet in the stirrups. I then had to find the doctor and his exam room nurse. I sure didn't want any surprises for them when they opened that exam room door!

Thankfully, the doctor on duty was one of our more compassionate ones. He agreed to do the exam but asked (with a smirk) if I had any preference on just what I'd like him to swab for the cervical cancer test. (This unkind, smart-aleck question came from our empathetic male doctor. The others who worked with us—you don't even want to know what their reaction would have been!) I suggested that he could just swab whatever he found in that area. While the exam was going on, I was on the phone arranging for this young man's follow-up counseling.

After the free counseling was arranged, and while I waited for my sad, confused patient, I thought about the need I had just two weeks earlier to have the words handed to me. Those Nebraska instructors were right, and they had actually taught me a Life Lesson. *When you truly understand what is needed and why, the words and the actions will be there. You will know how to "walk the talk." You need to ask the right questions, and then listen carefully with both your ears and your eyes for the "what and why." The words will come.*

I suspect that this is an example of the ability and willingness to listen to, accept, and then react empathetically to others that may be gender-specific. Most women that I know would accept that the young man's angst was both real and agonizing for him, even if every woman hearing it did not fully understand it. I know a few men who would also respect his pain—but very few. A majority of men appear to have a challenge in accepting or even attempting to understand something or someone who is very different from them. *"It is not like me, therefore I reject that it's real or important."* This is just a commentary. It falls into the category of the details of "things that woman do better than men" that we weren't going to get hung up about.

Ask Questions First, Act Second

Asking questions is the first thing that leaders do whenever they have any kind of leadership opportunity. In most cases, if you don't ask, the answers will not be readily offered up. You already know this from your personal life. How many times have you played Twenty Questions with kids to find out what's really going on? It's not that much different at work. The questions are a little harder, and the people you have to ask are a little bigger and older. But, if you don't drill down for the what and why the same way you do at home, you will be an unhappy (and likely unsuccessful) leader.

Knowing exactly what leaders are supposed to do starts with identifying what kind and how much leadership is required in a given situation and why. Once you are clear on what's needed and why your contribution is desirable and valuable, the answer to how to focus your leadership talents and energy appropriately will become much clearer. If you want to walk into a black hole without knowing why, that's your choice. But as a leader, you definitely don't want to bring along a group of followers with you!

This may seem like no-brainer advice: Know what and why first before you look at how. It may be pretty basic counsel, but too often it doesn't happen this way. Sometimes emerging leaders are so pleased about being given a position of responsibility that their enthusiasm overrides their good sense. This is not a good thing, but it is a normal, common reaction. These eager beavers jump into action without questioning only to find out that the action didn't match the "what and why." When this situation occurs, and if they find out they've been headed down the wrong path, these women need to know how to change or reverse direction quickly, or it may be their last opportunity to jump. Too-early leaping into action often equals a too-early leadership death.

Another headed-for-failure phenomenon that occurs is that decisions to move forward on...whatever, and requests for and commitments to leadership, don't always come with the reasons. Sometimes it's because the people making the decisions haven't thought whatever-it-is all the way through. Think about how many times in your work life that thought processes (of others, presumably) jump immediately from "We want to do....whatever" to "This is how we should do it." There's minimal mental distance between the short statements of desire and the plans for execution. Entire teams of people often get mired in the details of how-to-do when the what-to-do and why-we're-doing-it haven't even been validated. And you're supposed to know what you need to do to lead....whatever this is? That's not exactly a map for your success!

Here's an example of a too-quick leap to action. (This is real life. I have seen this almost exact scenario happen multiple times to several frustrated leaders.) You are told by someone who leads you (manager, supervisor, boss...someone) that the company wants to implement new software for recruiting and hiring processes and that you will be the project leader. You know the name of the software package and the expected start and end dates and budget for the project. You are told that the reason for the automation of the recruiting and hiring processes is to "increase efficiency and allow us to save time and money by doing more with less." You are advised to determine how many people you need for your team and who they are, and your leader will "see what he can do" to get their time. At this point, you should have many questions about why and what:

▶ *What is driving the need for increased efficiency? Just how inefficient are we now—and how do we know that we are? What will constitute improvement?*

▶ *Is a massive hiring initiative coming up, or are we planning to lay off people in HR to do "more with less." Less what—people, time, or money?*

▶ *Does this project include changing the processes we have now, or are we just automating what we do today?*

▶ *What are the chances of getting my team members full time, or will they be expected to add this in to their other jobs?*

▶ *And while we're talking about possibly conflicting schedules...is this an add-on responsibility for me?*

▶ Lots more questions...to determine what and why

The chance of getting all the information you need for the exact what and why for your leadership in the first request is slim. (It's likely that the requester doesn't have the answers because he hasn't thought up the questions. He's not doing the job...you are. It's up to you to figure out how.) If you don't ask, you won't know the words to lead with. Discovering the answers to the what and why questions after you've started and made commitments to your team leads to seriously ugly consequences. Your messaging to your team and to others in the company will be off-point and may even be misleading. You may be perceived by others as a weak, untrustworthy, uninformed leader.

If you are the one hearing the request and preparing to lead— you must, almost immediately, determine the **exact what and why** of what you'll be heading up. If you are the woman giving the leadership assignment to someone else, have the answers ready or find them quickly. You want to make sure that your anointed leader has everything she needs to be successful. Also realize that the questioning you are hearing from your newly-selected leader is an indicator that you've made the right choice. Real leaders question. She's questioning for maximum clarity...she may very well be the leader that will accomplish what you need. Don't be irritated by her questions—pat yourself on the back. You may have made a wise decision in selecting her.

Once you've determined the why, it's time to take action and do what leaders do. To help determine the what-to-do, we should start with examining more closely how leaders are. We already looked at this list a few times. Here it is again. Leaders are:

- ► Enthusiastic and passionate
- ► Trustworthy and honest
- ► Authentic and respectful in their approach to others
- ► Comfortable and calm with change or ambiguity
- ► Confident
- ► Brave

Presumably, good leaders then talk and walk in ways that are driven by possessing these traits. The leadership objectives of these characteristics would be to do the following:

► Build and maintain **enthusiasm and passion** in others

► Make people want to start and continue to follow you because you have been **trustworthy and honest** with others

► Engage and involve followers sincerely and appropriately because you are **authentic with and respectful** to others

► Provide **comfort and calm** to others in times of change or ambiguity so that others can be accepting of the changes around them

► Inspire others to be **confident** of your direction and also help build the followers' personal confidence

► Take the calculated risks that others may not be ready to try, and then provide the support so that followers may also be as **brave** as you are

So, just what exactly do leaders **do** in order to accomplish all these wonderful objectives?

CHAPTER 7

Nothing Happens Until You Sell Something

*Leaders build and maintain **enthusiasm and passion** in others.*

THERE APPEARS TO be a large number of people who believe that "selling" is a four-letter word. "Selling" for some people is an obscenity that conjures up visions of trickery and deceit, along with lies and manipulation to make sure that they never get anything for the "best price." The image of a sales person that immediately occurs to these people is a loud and boisterous person wearing a bright plaid suit selling a "mint" used car that you just know had to have been recovered from a flood.

Selling is, in fact, **not** a four-letter word. Leadership begins with selling something: yourself, your ideas, and your plans. This is selling for a worthy outcome. Others need to know why they should care. What are the benefits to them if they buy into your ideas? What do they have to invest and what are the risks? Most importantly, they need to know that **you** care. People will rarely do anything willingly or well if their leader doesn't care passionately about what she or he is leading. Your followers' appropriate levels of excitement, enthusiasm, and passion are built from the excitement, enthusiasm, and passion that you bring to your initiatives.

Life Lesson #9: Step Right Up!

My first and only attempt to learn to ride a motorcycle resulted in an ugly one-bike accident. In less than three minutes, that joyful wind-in-my-helmeted-face experience destroyed my right knee and sentenced me to years of surgeries, therapy, medication, and walking with crutches or a cane. My first lesson from the experience was, *"You should not try to do this again."*

I spent the next almost thirty years looking for the right doctor and the magic fix. Although I had seen more than a dozen doctors in many cities and clinics over the years, I could not find a doctor I trusted completely, and I just wasn't really ready to face the trauma of the fix, which included a total knee replacement. I was definitely hurting, but not enough to embrace the pain of the fix.

Finally, all the planets aligned and I was ready. The pain was no longer tolerable. I was tired of my well-worn, battle-scarred, 25-year-old cane, and I had good health insurance.

I began another search through all the doctors in Las Vegas who accepted my insurance, which seemed like the place to start to find the right one. I "interviewed" and discarded five orthopedic surgeons in a row. I wasn't inordinately concerned about their ability to perform the surgery. After all, an incredible number of knees have been replaced. All those doctors probably knew how to do it. It was no longer a ground-breaking, experimental procedure. My selection criteria included caring about me. I've always figured that spending my healthcare money should get me doctors who are technically proficient and, just as important, they should also be kind. Kindness does not seem to be a universal trait of orthopedic surgeons.

Serendipitously, I came across Dr. Michael Crovetti who owns and heads up Crovetti Orthopaedics and Sports Medicine in Las Vegas. From my first visit, I felt comforted and warmed by Dr. Crovetti's attention to my needs. The waiting room was beautiful and spotlessly clean. The magazines were up-to-date. The basket of treats on the front desk had really good stuff. Then the most amazing thing happened. I received apologies from two of his staff because I had to wait ten minutes past my appointment time! When I finally met Dr. Crovetti, his respectful demeanor and his enthusiastic (but realistic) approach and recommendations confirmed my initial impression. I had come to the right place. I was sold on the "concept" of the surgery and on Dr. Crovetti!

He performed the long-overdue surgery. It went quickly and efficiently, just the way he had carefully explained to me. It was after the surgery that I witnessed how really good Dr. Crovetti is at what he does—not only in the field of medicine, but also as a businessman. In a field of many surgeons to choose from, it's difficult to be professionally (read: financially) successful if people don't know and believe that you are good at what you do. Doctors need to get the word out. The most solid (and cheapest) advertising is through happy patients.

There is a second challenge for the success of an orthopedic surgeon. The patient is greatly involved in the ultimate success of the procedure. If the patient won't "cooperate" and won't work very hard to use and benefit from whatever it is she's received, the patient will not end up being happy and will not refer other patients, and the doctor will not be successful. Dr. Crovetti is and deserves to be financially successful. (That's probably why he can afford the good treats at the front desk!) This is what happened that speaks eloquently to the reasons for his success (besides the knee that works so well):

▶ The afternoon of the surgery, a cart with several potted plants appeared in my hospital room. The nurse told me that Dr. Crovetti always sends plants to all of his patients, right after surgery. I've probably told two dozen people about that. I never got anything from a doctor before except the bill!

▶ My in-hospital treatment for the first week included two daily visits to physical therapy. The first day during the first session, the therapists reviewed the list of at-home equipment with my therapy group of 10 people. Some of the equipment was required and some was optional, except for Dr. Crovetti's patients. *"Dr. Crovetti insists that all of his patients have all the equipment that we're showing you."* The therapists repeated the *"Dr. Crovetti insists...for his patients"* part so many times that one of my group said, *"I think I should have had Crovetti!"* I smiled (a little superior) because my right choice had been validated. There's nothing like a little envy from others to make you feel better about something.

▶ On the day after the surgery, Dr. Crovetti and I had a small confrontation about his standard protocol for therapy. The rule was that I would use a walker for a week (maybe two) and then graduate to a cane. After one day on the walker, I knew that I would not do that again. I was ready to "graduate" immediately. The other hospital staff in the room immediately protested my insistence about discarding the walker. Dr. Crovetti stopped them, re-stated my request, and negotiated a resolution. He said, *"I think we need to listen. She's used that cane for so many years that she's really good with it. Maybe she can go right to the cane."* He said he would approve the change in protocol if the therapists tested and approved my ability to be stable on the cane. The other stipulation was that if I passed the test, I must only use the cane where the others in the therapy group did not see it. (Dr. Crovetti didn't want open mutiny by any others who hated their walkers.) A doctor who listened and assumed that I knew what I was talking about, while still not just giving in! Another amazing thing! (I passed the therapists' tests and went right to the cane. I felt powerful and victorious!)

▶ I returned home, and all the equipment arrived. I was not just handed a prescription with directions to find the Medical Supply store that is never located where you can find it easily. Dr. Crovetti's own people brought the equipment to me and carefully went through the directions in my own setting. They told me that, *"Dr. Crovetti wants to make sure that you can handle everything at home. He would never just leave you on your own."* Nice.

▶ The home health nurse and the physical therapist began to appear every day, checking and exercising, and listening to my *"Is it supposed to look like this? Why does it feel weird over here too?"* concerns. The nurse told me that when a new staff member joins her home health company, they all go to Dr. Crovetti's office to spend the day with his staff, meet him personally, and understand his philosophy and approach to caring for his patients. She said he was the only doctor who did that. How smart is that for him to do? Of course, the nurse and therapist both sang his praises and again validated that he was the right choice!

I followed Dr. Crovetti's leadership and did what he encouraged me to do because he provided the right "sell" to build enthusiasm in me. I worked hard at my own recovery, which meant that I was successful, and subsequently he was too. I've also referred several patients to him. I usually say, *"Yes, he really knows his stuff—I'm sure lots of them do. But let me tell you about the plant I got from him."*

Are these exactly the right reasons for choosing a doctor? There are likely decent arguments that they are not. However, they were right for me, and for the two others I referred who are now Dr. Crovetti's satisfied patients!

I received more than a new knee (and a potted plant) from Dr. Crovetti. He also provided a powerful demonstration of a valuable Life Lesson: *Build the enthusiasm in others to follow you and to succeed before you attempt to lead them. Keep reinforcing that passion by selling right through to a successful conclusion!*

Sell to Lead With Passion and Excitement

Selling to lead is more complex than selling the latest electronic gadget. When a person buys what you as a leader are selling, they have to do something beyond just swiping their credit card. You are asking them to spend something even more valuable than their cash—you are asking them to spend their time, effort, focus, and regard. You may be asking them to take personal and/or professional risks to follow your lead. You are asking them to be personally vested in something that you care about. You are asking them to be enthusiastic and passionate with you.

Almost 25 years ago, my husband Bill was trying to build the enthusiasm in me so that I would follow his lead down the aisle and get married. He was selling but I was not buying. I wasn't resisting **him**; I was pushing back on the whole "let's get married" idea. I had already been married twice before and had found very little in the condition of matrimony to get too enthusiastic about.

A large group of friends were discussing (arguing) about how "Liz" and "Tony" should redecorate their new house. The most contentious discussion was around the master bedroom. Most of the men agreed with Tony and favored testosterone-driven metallic black and white with red accents. Liz and the rest of the women were leaning heavily toward apricot and minty green with lots of pillows in varying shades of those colors. While this was going on, Bill was silent but his body language said he strongly disagreed with....something.

I turned to sports-loving, hunting and camping, work-on-his-car-every-weekend Bill and asked what kind of master bedroom he preferred. He answered quietly, *"Well, I prefer a feminine bedroom. You know—pink with lacy stuff and lots of fancy pillows. I like to wake up in the morning and instantly know that I'm in a woman's bedroom"*

The conversation ceased momentarily while some "process-ing" (from very different perspectives) happened for everyone. I thought, *"That's about the sexiest thing I've ever heard!"* One of Bill's single friends said, *"Damn, Bill! I'm going to use that line!"* Tony turned to Liz and said, *"Yeah, apricot sounds good."* My girl-friends just stared at him and then at me.

That night, when my best friend was leaving, she told me, *"Oh, by the way, just so you know—if you drop over dead right this minute, I will step over your still-warm body to be first in line to get to him."*

Bill and I have been married for almost 25 years, and we think we're still on our honeymoon. Our bedroom is pink and lacy.

Building enthusiasm and passion in others—"selling" them on you and your ideas so that they are eager to follow—starts with listen-ing to the people who you want to lead. Why would they want to fol-low you for whatever reason you're leading them? What do they care about? What are their concerns about their work or the new initiative? What have they said or done that tells you what will inspire them to follow you, their inspired leader?

Determining the most effective way to encourage enthusiasm in others requires finding out what they care about—not what you think they might like or what someone else tells you.

When I was just barely old enough to vote, I ran for a seat on our small town council. I needed a "platform" and an advisor (male) suggested that I endorse a leash law. I accepted his advice without question and pitched, *"Vote for Jeanne, and I'll stop those dogs from running loose through your neighborhoods."* The problem with the platform was that my advisor was the only person who wanted dogs on leashes, and specifically, only his next-door neighbor's dog. Unknown to me at the time, everyone else in our town figured it was a dog's God-given right to run free. I lost the election.

Sometimes the answers are fairly easy to hear. If you are leading a local La Leche organization, it's likely true that all the members will follow with a passion to help ensure the health of children. If you want to be the sheriff in a community with a widespread burglary problem, people are more apt to build enthusiasm for your campaign if you have a strong plan to solve the problem and catch the burglars. Building enthusiasm in others is much easier when they are already fired up about whatever it is you are leading them toward.

But what do leaders do when their followers (or potential followers) are not as transparent about what they care about? How do they figure out what will inspire their followers? Most often, the clues are in the little things.

Figure Out What They Want to Buy...and Why

Asking your family to make their "Christmas Wish List" is the same type of approach you'd use to find out what the people you are planning to lead care about. If you want to know more about your family's needs and expectations than just their gift list, listening carefully to their answers will give you clues about other festive ideas you may have as well. If your plan for Christmas includes your children preparing baskets of toys and other goodies for homeless children, you will get clues about how easy the sell will be when you see their own lists. A child with a huge wish list of expensive toys may have to be sold a little harder on the idea of giving up something than a child who includes a request for their sibling or friend on their list. It would be good to know this information to plan your sales pitch before you introduce the idea! You may need to dig a little deeper to determine what will make your children want to follow your lead. You need to find out what they really care about first.

However, what if the followers are not your children? Then how do you find out what they care about? You ask, and then you listen to the answers. I will share with you a technique that I've used successfully many times in my career. I ask, *"What rings your bell"*? I have posed this question, with these exact words, on several different occasions to the people who were reporting to me. Because I've held various leadership positions in several different industries throughout my career, I've had the opportunity to hear the answers from a diverse group of people in widely varying environments. I've asked construction workers, teachers, consultants, government workers, and retail employees. I asked because I wanted to know what would build motivation, enthusiasm, and passion in them. I needed to know what they cared about so that I could lead them effectively.

When I decided to ask for this information the first time, I shared the idea with my peers. Their responses were immediate, quite vocal, and overwhelmingly negative. *"You'd better not ask that! People are going to ask for more money and then what will you do? You're probably going to hear requests for things that you can't deliver!"* My reply was, *"If I hear 'money,' then I have a bigger problem. I already have dissatisfied employees if money is the only reason they care about their jobs. If that's all that motivates them, I'll need to know that too. Then I'll have to deal with their overall unhappiness first."*

Professional and brave leadership response, wasn't it? That's what they heard me say. Inside, I was **really** worried about what I'd hear the first time I posed the question! I asked everyone being polled to return their responses to me in writing within 48 hours. Within 24 hours, I had already received answers from 21 of the 23 people who I asked. (I had never before seen such immediate responsiveness to anything I had asked from this group!) I had determined not to open the responses until I had all 23 of them. (I never did receive response number 23. When the deadline passed, I went to the person personally to inquire about why he had not responded. He replied curtly, *"I* *choose not to participate.*" That answer gave me all I needed to hear. He had already quit his job in his mind. I received his formal resignation three weeks later.)

With 22 responses in hand, I sat at home alone with a comforting chocolate bar (several of them, actually) and apprehensively began to read.

Not one response contained anything that I could not easily deliver! They were the simpler things that spoke to what was in my group's hearts—what they really cared about. They were requests for things that would make my group feel good about themselves and what they were doing.

I don't have and can't remember all 22 of those first responses. I do, however, remember some notable examples from the several times I've asked, *"What rings your bell?"*

I've heard:

> ▶ *I want the biggest hammer on the crew—a 16-ounce one. I'll buy it myself if I have to. I just want it.* (Obviously a construction worker. A 16-ounce hammer was not "standard issue" since very few carpenters could actually handle one that heavy. The hammers had previously been banned because they often caused more damage than good. I bought him the hammer.)

> ▶ *I really like it when I've said something good and you look at me sideways and wink.* (This answer came from a professional consultant who often said very good things.That was certainly easy to accommodate. I could remember to wink every time she said something good!)

► *I would like to have printed certificates when I've met my sales quota or when I've received good customer comments—times like that. And, I'd like you to give them to me in front of the other employees.* (This was from the manager of a florist shop, part of a group of stores that I was re-building after an economic downturn. I could definitely write, print, and award certificates!)

► *What really rings my bell is when your husband Bill comes to the school and you ask me to join the two of you for dinner.* (I wasn't sure if this Director of Education liked going to dinner with me, or if my husband Bill was really the draw for her. Either way worked for me. I made sure that she was often invited to dinner.)

It is possible that you could ask your followers what rings their bell and not be totally delighted with the responses you receive. But you need to hear the less-than-wonderful answers too! All the answers you receive will help you know what is needed to build and maintain enthusiasm and passion in others.

After you find out what they care about, you will then need to employ all of your other leadership skills to finish the job of building and maintaining enthusiasm in others. You will want to make sure that you are trustworthy and honest, authentic and respectful, comforting and calm, and confident and brave while you build and foster the passion in others.

Sell the Changes

The bottom line of leadership is that a leader changes things with new ideas, new initiatives, new ways of governing, and new direction. The leader of a basketball team may change the attitude of the players to increase the drive and the desire to come together as a team to win. The leader of a school board may work to effect change in policy. To change things, you must first sell others on the idea that the change is good—for them first, and then for others.

Selling is to effect change in something—process, behaviors, attitudes. It's all about getting others to invest in you, in your ideas, and in themselves. Selling to deliver on superior leadership is definitely not a negative phrase. It is the practical application of the need to build and maintain enthusiasm and passion in those who will follow you.

Closely related to selling, and absolutely required, is the next leadership trait that all good leaders exhibit: being trustworthy and honest.

CHAPTER 8

Can You Handle the Truth?

*Leaders make people want to start and continue to follow them because they have been **trustworthy and honest** with others.*

THIS SOUNDS LIKE the memorable Jack Nicholson line from the 1992 movie *A Few Good Men:* "Truth? You can't handle the truth!"[10]

You would think that the leadership requirement to be trustworthy and honest would be so obvious that we wouldn't even have to discuss it. *"Of course I can handle the truth."* The reality is that knowing exactly what the truth is, relative to leadership action, is not clearly black and white. There are several factors that contribute to the ambiguous elements of trustworthiness and honesty:

1. You made a commitment to the people you lead that you can no longer honor.

---

[10] The line "You can't handle the truth!" was voted the twenty-ninth greatest American movie quote of all time by the American Film Institute. According to the *Guinness Book of Film*, the number one quoted movie line is from the 1962 movie *Dr. No*. That line is "...Bond. James Bond." I wonder if it's because it's easy to remember or if we all secretly (regardless of gender) would like to be James Bond.

2. It is often not totally clear to you what the truth about a situation is.

3. The "unvarnished" truth may stand in the way of accomplishing what has to be done.

4. Today's truth becomes just a vague memory tomorrow. Circumstances may have changed, which means that the truth has changed.

There are a few more circumstances that contribute to the "thin air" in which trustworthiness and honesty sometimes reside, but we can start with examining these four.

1.   **You made a commitment to the people you lead that you can no longer honor.** For example: You asked for, and believed that you had received authorization for, an extra day off that would not be charged against accrued vacation time for your team if they successfully completed the project on time. The on-time completion of the project will be next week, and you mention to your supervisor that your department will be closed on the following Friday for the "On-Time Day." You hear, *"What are you talking about? I never authorized that."* Or you may hear, *"We can't let that happen. We have an important client presentation to prepare for and we need those people to work on it. They've been so tied up with this project that they need to get back to business right away."* But your team trusted you when you made the commitment to the day off! Now what?

What do leaders do? You have a number of approaches to try. You can:

▸ **Remind the person** (in this case, your supervisor) **gently and quietly** of the conversation or e-mail that verified that permission was given for the day off. It is possible that he doesn't remember the authorization. It's not likely, but it is possible. Taking a default attitude that your leader would not knowingly go against his word to you is an honorable thing to do because it gives him an opportunity to recover from his denial stance. If he has chosen not to remember and does intend to break his word to you, however, an aggressive approach on "proof" may not be well received and may end up being your last opportunity to change your leader's mind. You don't want to have the door closed on this conversation right from the beginning. If your supervisor recants when he hears or sees the "not-in-his-face" proof, then the discussion is over and a sincere, *"Thanks! I'm sure they will all appreciate what you've done for them,"* is appropriate. Then leave—quickly before he changes his mind again!

If the proof does not remind your supervisor that he once gave this authorization, or if he says it doesn't matter because he's taking the permission back, then you'll want to move on to another approach option.

▶ **Appeal to his preference for a positive public image.** If your supervisor's objection is still that he never authorized the day off, take the high road and apologize for your misunderstanding. Tell him what may be a variation of the truth: *"Arrgghh…I misspoke to my people then. I've already told them that you wanted them to have this day off and had suggested it to me as a fitting reward for all the extraordinary effort they put into this. Can you help me figure out how to reverse this without either of us losing face with them?"* Yes, if this is not **exactly** what you told your people, then this approach is not totally honest. However, no harm, no foul here. Even if it's not word-for-word, you definitely want to speak the "variation" to your supervisor with a sincere and completely straight face. If you can't do that, then don't try this approach! The situation will only get worse if your supervisor suspects that you are only flattering him. The appeal to a positive image will work in a large percentage of these "denial" situations. If it doesn't, though, try another tactic.

▶ **Negotiate for a satisfactory compromise.** Could all agendas and expectations be served if half of the people took off next week and the other half the week after that? Can you get back to your supervisor with a plan to ensure that nothing falls through the cracks or gets delayed because of the day off? Can you run some numbers to make sure that the company will not lose money because of the day off? Show that you are willing to put forth effort to satisfy what you both want. Negotiating to reach a mutually acceptable resolution will also often work in these situations.

If your attempt at negotiating with your supervisor doesn't fix things, then you must undo with your people what you had previously set in place. Take a deep breath, be brave, and tell them the truth as it was told to you—whether or not you have fully accepted it yourself. The truth might be as follows: *"I believed that I had gone through the proper channels to get permission for the 'On-Time Day,' but I just found out that I had not. Although I attempted to fix my mistake, it is now too late and I could not get the authorization. I'm sorry that I inadvertently misled you. I certainly never meant to do that, and I will make sure that I do things right the next time. We won't be taking the 'On-Time Day' next week. I hope that this change doesn't interfere horribly with any plans you may have already made. Is there something I can do for any or all of you to help take the sting out of this?"*

Or the truth could be as follows: *"I have learned that there is a strategic client presentation that needs serious attention. My boss believes that the presentation won't go well unless you people are the ones working on it. That's what comes sometimes when you are really good at what you do! I need to cancel our 'On-Time Day' because right now you are really needed to stay on the job and get the presentation out the door. I hope that this doesn't interfere horribly with any plans you may have already made. Is there something I can do for any or all of you to help take the sting out of this?"* If your supervisor has indicated that there's a possibility to schedule the On-Time Day at another time, you may choose to share that with your team. Just a word of caution—make sure that you truly believe that the day off can happen before you announce it. You certainly don't want to have to repeat the, *"Sorry, it's not going to happen,"* again!

In this situation, the following is what leaders do **not** do:

▶ Pitch a fit with the boss and insist that because he told them it would, On-Time Day **is** going to happen. (With this approach, you may have just wrapped a noose around your neck!)

▶ Go over the boss's head.

▶ Tell your people that Mr. Killjoy (a.k.a., the boss) is going back on his word and that you tried to "save" them, but he won't back down.

2.   **It is often not totally clear to you what the "truth" about a situation is.** For example: You are the head of your company's Human Resources Department. You've been told to organize a team of people to review all the business processes that are currently in use.

The objective of this task, as it was explained to you, is to remove some of the burden and frustration from the people who report to you. The stated goal is to allow people to focus on more "value-added" services and initiatives by being more efficient and effective in their day-to-day operations. You have also heard that there are budget cuts coming up. Is the truth a desire to create a better work environment in order to add innovative projects or is it a prelude to laying off people? How do you present the message, whatever it may be, and maintain being trustworthy and honest with your people?

What do leaders do?

> ▶ **Try to validate what the whole truth really is.** Ask a trusted supervisor if there is another reason behind the process review initiative. It is very important to have this discussion privately! Give the supervisor a valid reason for questioning what you were told officially. *"This question and your answer are strictly 'off the record.' I would not disclose any additional information that you tell me when I'm explaining this to my team. I'm asking this to make sure I'm prepared for their questions in case they've also heard the same rumors and are worried about their jobs. I believe this is an important initiative and want to make sure that my team is enthusiastic about working on it and that we get a good result. If there is thought about laying off some of them after the review, then I will know not to emphatically deny that possibility if I'm asked. I would tell them that I have not seen anything that says the objectives are other than I've explained. I would state that I am supportive of the project and ask for their enthusiastic participation."*

► If the answer is that there could be layoffs, then you'll want to **approach your team the way you told the supervisor you would.** (Trustworthiness and honesty have to go up the chain as well as down!) If the answer is that there are no layoffs anticipated, you are within the boundaries of honesty to answer that way if you are asked. *"I have been told that there are no layoffs anticipated."*

In this situation, the following is what leaders do **not** do:

► Challenge the reasons in a group setting. You would be publicly calling someone a liar and you may not get the whole truth anyway. (Here comes that noose around your neck again!)

► Indicate in any way to your people that you don't believe that what you were told is the whole truth. Statements such as, *"Well, that's what they told me, but who knows,"* are not leadership comments.

3.   **The "unvarnished" truth may be counterproductive to accomplishing what has to be achieved.** For example: You are preparing to roll out a new process in your organization to oversee the quality of the project managers' work. The process will allow additional visibility and more formal oversight of the project managers' activities to ensure that they are following the rules and processes that are in place. Reports, client deliverables, and other project documents will each be monitored and reviewed to ensure that they are all on time and of the quality that is expected and required. If the agreed-to deadlines are not being met, or the project managers' work is professionally substandard in any way, a discrepancy report will be given to them and

to their supervisors to help ensure future compliance. Because of the remote nature of the work and the challenges that have arisen in trying to ensure consistent, quality services to all clients, formalizing the monitoring process is a much-needed change.

What do leaders do?

Life Lesson #10: Coming Up Roses!

Many years ago when my children were pre-school age, I was blessed with an excellent full-time babysitter/housekeeper named Dorothy who came to our house every day, while I worked (a little more than) full time. She did it all: watched the girls, cleaned the house, ordered the groceries, did the laundry, and started dinner. (Not the best cook in the world, but I was not about to complain!) Life was definitely good.

We moved into a new house, and Dorothy had worked tirelessly to help us get settled in. A week after our big move, Dorothy called me at work. I immediately took her call even though I had to step out of an important meeting at the time. Dorothy never called me at work unless there was some kind of emergency. I had a hard time focusing on what she was saying at first because of the strong mental image that my youngest and most daring child was probably in an ambulance on the way to the emergency room. I did manage to pull myself together, however, and I will never forget the conversation.

Dorothy: *"We are going to have a really great garden at this new house! I already called the nursery and ordered six flats of flowers. They're going to bring them tomorrow, and I'll start planting them."*

Flowers—she called me at work about flowers? Not likely.

Jeanne: *"How do you know that we're going to have a great garden?"*

Dorothy: *"We have the best black dirt I've ever seen! Just wait 'til you see it! Everything's going to grow good in this dirt!*

What black dirt? I hadn't seen any. There was grass everywhere.

Jeanne: *"How do you know we have such good dirt? I haven't seen any."*

Dorothy: *"Oh, the water line to the house broke. There's a big back-hoe here digging up the whole yard. They think they can fix it, but they're not sure if they can finish today. But you should just see that black dirt. As soon as they're done, I'm going to be planting flowers! We're going to have a great garden!"*

After my heart starting beating again, I managed to croak out, *"Thanks for letting me know, Dorothy. I'm sure the garden will be wonderful. I'll probably be home a little earlier tonight."*

She told me the truth. She just knew she needed to try to make the message go down a little easier. She also handed me a Life Lesson: *When you have a difficult message to deliver, come up with a truthful statement that will also help "the medicine go down."*

Tell the Truth With a Carrot and a Stick

Our oversight rollout example is one in which complex leadership actions are required. (You may want to review Chapter 7: Nothing Happens Until You Sell Something.) There is a fine line (too often crossed to the wrong side by faux leaders) between telling the truth and putting an appropriate "spin" on something to help make the message go down. A leadership spin is not deceitful or dishonest or shrouded in trickery. Finding the right spin means addressing a likely less-than-thrilling change in a way that allows people to overcome their immediate resistance. It gives them a reason and time to examine and then subsequently accept the change and the whole truth. You don't need to hit them in the head with the truth, however—you can lead in to it. If you are going to introduce a "stick," you will also want to find the "carrot" and lead with the carrot first.

Carrot in hand, you can move forward with the specifics of what leaders do.

> ► **They recognize and accept the truth** about the probability of immediate acceptance of the new process by the project managers—the participants in the process who will be most impacted by the oversight procedures. It is likely that the project managers will not immediately embrace the new process. Just because this is a good thing for the company, the project managers will not be delighted to hear about another layer of review and more compliance requirements. Don't lie to yourself. This is not going to be an instantly- applauded message.

> ► **Figure out what it will take to make the message and compliance with the process more "digestible."** A successful lead-in is **not**, *"We are concerned about the quality of project management that you are providing, so we are*

going to put a formal oversight process in place to ensure that you are complying with the rules." So, what is the better message? Ask yourself what in the new process might appeal to the project managers. Then listen to your own answer from their perspective, not yours.

Seek and listen to feedback from one or two managers. Ask them the same question about what in the process might appeal to the other project managers. It's not a good idea to ask a large number of them. The responses may get too "noisy" and confusing because there are too many answers, or they may believe that you are asking for consensus agreement on whether or not to implement the new process. In this situation, you are not asking for their "permission;" you are asking for help in how to roll out the process in a way that ensures its effectiveness.

▶ **Determine how you can incorporate** into the process and the messaging **a few carrots** that you or your manager advisors have suggested. These carrots could be that you agree to provide additional training for the managers to make sure they fully understand what is required because you want to make sure that they are *"well positioned to be successful."* You may integrate an administrative function into the process that will allow someone else to prepare the templates for the project documents, with the specific client logos and names for example, so that the project managers can spend their time on more value-added aspects of their job. Find the carrots and lead with them in your messaging.

▶ **Be honest and forthright about the stick in the message and process.** Let the project managers know that a significant element in the process is the monitoring-to-compliance aspect. Just don't lead with this element. Don't start with, *"The yard is all dug up and it will probably cost you a fortune to fix the leak."* Instead, open with, *"We are going to have a really great garden!"* Then, honestly and completely, follow the opener with the rest of the message about all the objectives of the new process.

In this situation, the following is what leaders do **not** do:

- ► **Refuse to accept and incorporate the fact that people need more incentive than just "doing what is best for the company."** Poor leaders sometimes choose to deny this reality because it means they have to do more work themselves. They need to re-tool or make changes in what they already designed. They want to take a seemingly easier and quicker way. This is not good leadership.

- ► **Sugarcoat the real objective by hiding the less-than-savory parts and letting people find out later, when they've already accepted the good parts.** In this approach, the leader uses a spin as trickery. This never works out well. The leader has just shot herself in the foot for the future. The next time she tries to introduce something (either good or bad), she will have little credibility with or trust from her team.

- ► **Promise a carrot but do not deliver on it.** The ramifications of this approach should be obvious! If you offer something that you know is desirable in return for the support from others, be very sure that you can actually produce that carrot. If no carrots appear, your credibility will be seriously questioned for a very long time. People tend to have long

► memories when they feel they've been tricked.

4. Today's truth becomes just a vague memory tomorrow. Circumstances may have changed, which means that the truth has changed. This situation occurs so frequently in a dynamic world that good leaders become very practiced on how to respond to it and lead through it.

What do leaders do?

They tell the truth. They say, *"I had explained our situation and changes based on what we knew then. Now, other factors have altered our circumstance, which means that we need to be flexible in our approach. I appreciate the efforts you've expended in going down the path we were taking, but now we must switch directions to accommodate our new information and requirements. We certainly want to leverage what has already been accomplished for our new plans, and I'll be meeting with you to review how we can incorporate those ideas into our new mission."*

In these situations, the following is what leaders do **not** do:

► Blame someone else for the change in the direction, the plans, or the truth. If you are charged with crafting or delivering the message, then accept it yourself wholeheartedly. You need to deal with your own misgivings and change aversion in the privacy of your linen closet at home—not with your people.

► Apologize for the change in the message. Change is simply a reality of the dynamics of business. Apologizing makes the change appear to be a bigger deal than it really is.

> ► Refuse to acknowledge that your people may need time to "mourn" the potential loss of their efforts in listening to and following the old truth. Recognize that you've had more time to deal with the grief of the change because you've known about it longer. Give your people at least the same amount of time that you've had to mourn their loss.

The people with whom a leader must be trustworthy and honest include those who are following you, the people who you report to, your business partners, and your clients. The absolute requirement for trustworthiness and honesty extends to all people with whom you have a working relationship. It also means role modeling the trust and honesty that you expect and deserve to have from them. It means leading by example, so that all parties can learn and benefit from the relationship. In the category of truthfulness and honesty, you do get back what you deliver.

If You Say It, You Must Do It

Another element of the trustworthy and honest mandate is to do what you say you are going to do and what you ask of others. One of the problems with leaders who are OCD is that they often take on more than they should, and in doing so, try to make others do more than they can. Work every day to be honest with yourself about what you can and should be doing. You will have a greater chance of being realistic about what you expect from others. You will build more trust when you ask something from them; you have thought out the implications and believe that they can be successful. Let your team hear and see that you are willing and able to support them appropriately because you have your priorities aligned and your commitments well thought out and planned. Let them trust that what you are saying and leading toward can be done, and then lead the way by showing that you are willing to put forth the work as well.

Sometimes the honest and trusted answer is to just say, *"No."* There are times when people will ask for or expect leadership from you that you cannot or are not willing to give. For example, you may be asked too often to become someone's mentor. This is a significant commitment to which you may not have the time, the desire, or the ability to give. You may recognize that a mentoring relationship between you and the requesting individual would not work well because of any number of personal or professional reasons. It is more honest to decline the request and offer to help the person find the appropriate mentor. Or you may be asked to organize the next giant family reunion. If you know that you will not be able to give the task the time it needs to be completed correctly, it is more honest to thank the requestor for the trust she showed by believing you could do it. But don't take on the job if you know that you will not be able to follow it all the way through. When you couple the decline with an offer to assist the next selected family leader with a specific assignment, you will be more trustworthy in your ability to deliver because you've been honest in your response.

Your enthusiasm, passion, trustworthiness, and honesty are all absolutely required to provide the leadership to "make something happen." How will you leverage these valuable characteristics to make something happen? By paying attention to and doing the little things!

CHAPTER 9

Do the Little Things...Big Things Follow!

*Leaders engage and involve followers sincerely and appropriately because they are **authentic with and respectful** to others.*

THIS IS A great line from the movie **Steel Magnolias:** *The ability to accessorize is what separates man from the animals. And...the ability to accessorize well is what separates women from men.* Leadership is all about attention to the small things because both the devil and the angel—the bad and the good—reside in the details. Women understand about details.

Soon after Bill and I were married, I was a cooking dervish, preparing dinner for several guests that were arriving (too) soon. Bill offered to set the table and I accepted the offer, although I was a little concerned because I had not previously validated his skill in setting a "proper" table. In spite of my hesitation, I pointed to the stacks of my favorite Villeroy and Boch china—the set with the bright apricot and purple poppies that would complement my menu perfectly.

When Bill finished, I did my quality control check on his job and discovered that the apricot poppies were not all pointed the same way. Not a huge problem—I just turned each plate to line up the pattern perfectly. Bill was a little offended. *"What are you doing? What was wrong with the plates?"* I gently explained that, while his overall job was good, proper presentation requires having the patterns lined up. Wide-eyed, Bill threw his hands in the air in the universal sign of surrender. *"Okay, I don't get it, but I'll just go with it. But how about if we buy some dishes without a pattern? Wouldn't that be easier on both of us?"* At least he was wise enough not to go after my compulsion to point all the poppies in the same direction.

Being authentic and demonstrating respect for others go hand in hand, and they are all about the small things that, combined, demonstrate that you are real and that you care for others. You are providing quality leadership when you demonstrate that you recognize and accept the value of the people you lead and work toward providing a mental, emotional, and sometimes physical environment in which they feel comfortable and confident. When you place a high value on others, you know that there is only one proper way to treat them: with straightforward and honest respect given authentically. You will want to give the best of yourself to your team because they deserve it. (That's what drives my obsession with a "proper" table setting. My guests deserve the best I can give them—including lined-up poppies.)

I learned (painfully) the reality that the little things add up and bring big things, both good and bad.

Life Lesson #11: Veni, Vidi, Vici: Not!

I attended Ursuline Academy, an all-girls Catholic school in southeast Missouri, for seven years and graduated from the high school there. The Academy (sadly no longer in operation) had a huge, pastoral campus for an incredibly small student count. We had approximately 100 students in the entire school each year. With so few students, you could never just blend into the woodwork or the giant maple trees. Those nuns always had you on their radar! The school was firmly committed to academic excellence and to molding young women into Ursuline Girls. An Ursuline Girl exhibited the traits of "Courtesy, Honesty, and Courage." The staff was delighted with students who were hardworking, innovative, and spirited but was less than pleased when they had to deal with mavericks. I was all of those things. The Ursuline nuns and I had interesting times together.

I had successfully avoided taking Home Economics until my senior year and had no intention of ever attending the class. The head of the Academy, Mother Henrietta, had a different intention. In my curriculum-planning discussion (read: confrontation), I pulled out all the stops. I explained that I was requesting a trade of Home Economics class for the "greater academic endeavor" and opportunity to take Latin IV. I hastened to inform her that I already knew how to sew and cook because I had been in 4H for four years. But, as I explained to Mother Henrietta, the chance to continue studying with one of the finest Latin teachers in the country was priceless!

There were two problems with my proposal. One challenge was that Home Economics was required for graduation. I suggested that Mother Henrietta had both the wisdom and the power to "modify" those requirements in extraordinary circumstances. She nodded. It was a tiny nod and gone in a flash, but I saw it That nod told me that I had her on the line. Now I just had to reel her in.

The second problem was that there was no Latin IV class. There were no other students for fourth-year Latin. I expressed great surprise that Mother Henrietta would even consider denying a student, who was hungry for knowledge, the ability to learn because of a small problem like not having a class. I told her that I was requesting this honestly, courteously, and with courage. I was an Ursuline Girl and was begging for more Latin studies. I remember vividly concluding that particular argument with, "Please let me learn!" I was totally shameless. I did not intend to make an apron or bake cookies in Home Ec! I could tell Mother Henrietta was wavering.

Then I overplayed my hand. Our school participated in national testing for English, Math, and most of the Sciences. But I knew we had never sat for the National Latin Exam because the Academy had never "fielded" a "National Latin Scholar." I'm not sure how it happened exactly, but I implied that I would be that Latin Scholar. I would not only sit for the exam, I would also bring great prestige to the Academy because they would have produced the country's top high school Latin Scholar. Bingo! Mother Henrietta was sold—and in the joy of my victory, I promptly erased the Latin Scholar claim from my consciousness.

There we were for a year, just Mother Monica and me studying Latin. It was not an easy gig, and several times I regretted having won the battle! Sewing an apron didn't seem as awful as I had envisioned. One of the problems with being the only student in the class was that I always knew I was going to be called on. There was no chance Mother Monica would pick someone else to answer the questions. She also required that we only speak Latin in the class—no English was allowed! I questioned the practicality of that stipulation because, unless I worked at the Vatican, I'd likely never have anyone to talk to in Latin again. There was no dissuading Mother Monica, however. It was Latin or silence.

As the end of the year approached, Mother Monica began to talk about the National Latin Exam and started giving me way too many extra books to ensure that I was completely ready to test. She would ask me if I had studied the books. I didn't exactly lie—I was an Ursuline Girl. I said I thought they were "enlightening" and "allowed me to continue to grow." Yeah, right! My arm muscles were the only things growing from carrying around those huge volumes of seriously old Latin writings! I never actually opened them, though.

Because of our geographic distance from the testing center in Chicago, Mother Monica had received permission for me to take the exam at our school, while still being required to follow all the rules including the required timing of 9:30 a.m. to 12:30 p.m. She explained that there was going to be a proctor (not her) sitting in the room to ensure I didn't open any books or cheat in any other way. My attitude was, "Whatever..."

The day of the exam arrived. The first unusual thing that happened was that I was told that I was excused from my first class of the day so that I could "rest and contemplate" by strolling the campus or going anywhere else that I wanted to. I sauntered out of the morning General Assembly with a superior grin at my glaring classmates. I showed up in the Latin classroom promptly at 9:00 a.m. as I had been instructed to do. That's when I immediately noticed that things were very strange. There was a nun I had never seen before sitting in the corner. She was the proctor who had traveled from St. Louis (a distance of 100 miles) to satisfy the testing requirements. Mother Monica had a bottle of Coke sitting on my desk next to a glass with two ice cubes. She said that she was concerned that I might get thirsty during the test and wanted to give me the option of drinking from the bottle or using a glass. I had never seen Coke or water or anything in a classroom at the Academy! Drinking from a bottle! That was strictly forbidden! Mother Monica also had a plate of cookies (made that morning for me, she told me) in case I got hungry. She had a radio there and asked if I worked better with a little background sound, and if so, which station did I want to listen to? What was going on!? Mother Monica wanted to know if I wanted the window open or shut. She had never asked me that before! Why was she doing all of this for me?

Holding a huge stop watch in her hand and preparing to begin the test, she said quietly, *"We've never had the National Latin Scholar before."* My heart stopped beating as I suddenly remembered my overblown boast of being our school's first National Latin Scholar. That's what these extraordinary arrangements were about! I hadn't just said I would sit for the exam; I had committed to aceing it! I tested for three hours in a haze of remorse and shame.

About a month later, it was graduation day, which was preceded by the Rose Ceremony held the night before. At the Rose Ceremony, the top students in each class, as well as the national test participants in all fields of study, received their awards. Mother Henrietta explained that for the first time, the Academy had participated in the National Latin Exam, and she was proud to announce that Jeanne Erpenbach had the distinction of being one of the Top Ten High School Latin Scholars in America. I was *one* of the Top Ten. I was not *the* Latin Scholar. Mother Henrietta may have been pleased, but Mother Monica was not, and neither was I. I don't know if Mother Monica looked at me when she handed me the award or not; I couldn't bear to look up at her.

That was one of the more painful Life Lessons that I ever learned, and I have never forgotten it. Even now, over 40 years later, I feel tremendous pain with this memory. I made a commitment that I had no intention of honoring. I thought at the time that it was "no big deal." **I** didn't care about being a National Latin Scholar. But **they** cared—especially Mother Monica. This was a "little thing" that meant a great deal to someone else—a person who had worked hard to help me. My friends attempted to console me (and stop my crying) after the ceremony by saying that the distinction between number one and one of the top ten was really small. But I was not to be consoled, then or now. I knew that it wasn't a huge difference. But it was a little thing that meant the most to someone who trusted me and really needed that "little thing."

That was my initiation into this Life Lesson: *Understand and accept that it's almost never the big things that people need and look for us to provide. The people who we care about and lead look for, need, and deserve our regard and attention to the little things. The devil and the angel—the bad and the good—are in the details.*

Being "Real" is in the Details

What exactly does it mean to be authentic? What is needed to be or become more real with others? Sometimes we can all learn what to do by seeing what **not** to do.

▶ **Don't try to charm or give false flattery to people.** Respect others enough to believe that they'll know when they're being fed a dishonest line.

Many years ago a young and "charming" man (who needs to remain nameless) worked for me. He had aspirations of grandeur fueled by his good looks and his raconteur banter. He told me very seriously that he would own his own large, successful company and be a ready-to-retire, multi-millionaire by the time he was 35. All I needed to do for him was to pay $5,000 for his entrance into a local leadership program where he would get great visibility to all the established leaders who would open doors for him. (They would, of course, recognize his incredible talent as soon as they met him.) I asked what kind of successful company he intended to start and head up. I asked what his plans were to become both a successful leader and wealthy—besides my paying $5,000 for his desired visibility. I inquired about why he thought he would achieve his goals. What was his plan?

The young man's planning consisted of, *"It's very easy for me to make people like me. That's how I get what I want from them."* He explained that he knew how to appeal to what people wanted to hear, which, in turn, made them want to do things for him. He offered an example. *"When I was in college and helping in my mother's shop, whenever an older, gray-haired woman came in, I would call her a 'young lady.' They always liked that because they thought they didn't look old and that I was complimenting them. They probably thought that I was interested in them. That made them like me."* (Are you cringing when you read this?)

This approach was so wrong on so many different levels that I didn't even know where to begin! The young man's success plan was predicated on his ability to falsely flatter people and his willingness to believe that it was effective. I knew I had no words of wisdom that would dissuade him, so I didn't offer much teaching or leadership. I suggested that when he came up with a workable plan, he could make the $5,000 request again. He never did, and I never paid the $5,000.

A default position that is likely a correct one to take is that people who do not honestly engage with others are not honest themselves. They should not be trusted, or followed. Authentic means saying what you mean and what you believe is true—respectfully.

▶ **Don't brag about your less-than-savory characteristics.** Being authentic does not mean holding on to and advertising your own character flaws as though they are something good.

A statement that demonstrates misplaced pride in what others recognize as poor qualities is, *"I've just always been stubborn. That's just how I am."* Am I hearing correctly that you are close-minded and won't listen to new information once you've made a decision? Another statement that broadcasts a more complex flaw is, *"I've just never had any patience with people who won't work on their own shortcomings. If they don't want to help themselves, then I'm not willing to help them either."* Amazing! Just what have those people done to allow you to know that they don't want to help themselves? You have proof of that? I've just heard you tell me that you are judgmental and intolerant and that you are obviously blind to shortcomings in yourself. Therefore, I can assume that you are not willing to work on those shortcomings either!

You (and I) have heard some misguided women say, *"Yep, I'm a bitch. I always have been a bitch—that's just how it is."* Okay...if being a bitch is what's called for or desirable in a given situation, that'll work. But if it's not, then why advertise that particular quality?

Advertising (sometimes called with false modesty "owning up to") a flaw is not being honest. It's really being dishonest to yourself. It's delusional to believe that whatever we do is okay. It's much too self-centered to believe that being stubborn, intolerant, or combative is acceptable to others just because that's, *"How I am."*

Being respectful means listening to others whom you trust when you hear that you need to work on something in yourself. You may hear the need to become more open-minded, more collaborative, or more patient. Being authentic to ourselves includes accepting the reality that not every trait we possess is the best.

▶ **Don't believe that you can avoid admitting when you are wrong.** Being authentic and respectful to others means that you will often have to say, *"I'm sorry."*

Being respectful of others and authentic in your approach also means that you do not try to justify or make excuses for your mistakes. It includes not attempting to cover them up or blame others for them. It means calling out the elephant in the room: you were wrong. The reality is that leaders make many mistakes. If you count the number of things that they do wrong, the total will likely be much higher than the number of missteps made by the people they lead. Leaders take more chances, which translates to an increased opportunity to make mistakes. The number of times a leader is wrong is not the important metric. The more significant measurement is the percentage of the misses relative to the total number of tries. You want to make sure your "hit rate" of doing the right thing is much greater than the failure rate. If you have to admit to mistakes and say you're sorry more often than not, then there are other problems that need your immediate attention. Possibly you really don't know what you're doing in a specific circumstance and need to listen to and follow the counsel of others to get you on the right track. Never walk with your hands or head empty—we can all learn from others who are willing (and able) to help.

► **Don't spout platitudes or make false offers of support.** People who believe they are "providing leadership" by quoting too-often used and frequently trite phrases are not providing leadership. This approach is insulting to a person's intelligence when it is used, and it often carries long-term negative backlash. It is disrespectful.

Have you ever listened to someone talk and had to work hard to figure out if they really **said** anything? If you have to struggle to determine if they have, they likely have not. The person is either not being authentic, is not listening to or understanding the challenges, or is not prepared, which means that your time and attention were not being respected.

You have likely heard alleged leaders pontificate rather than listen and then respond to what they've heard. They seem to prefer to just offer words instead of carefully evaluating a situation and offering support that is pertinent, appropriate, and memorable. When the people they are leading hear the same phrases too often, they tune out and turn away from the leader. They have become conditioned to hearing, "Yaddah, Yaddah, Yaddah..." In time, the people hearing the empty words begin to merely tolerate the person (if they have to do even that) instead of having respect for and following him as a leader.

Some examples of platitudinous statements, along with common reactions to them, are as follows:

o *We're going to say what we'll do and do what we say.* And, just what would that be? I haven't heard you say what you'll do.

   o *Although we don't agree, I would fight to the death to
    defend your right to disagree.*
    Are you crazy? There's no way you'd die to let me tell
    you I don't think your plan is good.

   o *When the going gets tough, the tough get going.*
    Sure, and every time I've heard that it means that
    I'm the one who has to get going—not you.

Closely related to the unacceptability of empty phrases are the false offers of support. If you don't intend to help, then don't make the offer. (You already know this because you hate it when it happens to you. How do you feel about the person who has promised what never appeared?)

Years ago, when I was in the construction business, I had a woman partner (who needs to remain nameless). She knew and cared a lot about building and knew and cared very little about people. Our best foreman had been absent too often and had been uncharacteristically temperamental and not doing his usual fine work. I suggested to my partner that he may have some personal issues that were interfering with his work.

That morning after she distributed the day's roster of assignments, my partner said to our foreman (while looking down at her papers), "*It seems like you're upset about something. Listen, anytime you want to talk to me about what's wrong, just let me know.*" She continued to look down while our foreman stood there, obviously wanting to talk. He then turned to me with a sad look of rejection and resignation and just walked away. He had heard my partner's "empathy statements" before. He knew she had no intention of actually listening to his problems.

> The next week our foreman was given a particularly difficult job to lead, and he just quit on the spot. I knew that we had lost an excellent foreman at least in part because he could no longer tolerate hearing false statements of regard and support.

Just how does doing the little authentic and respectful things connect to achieving the larger successes in life?

Go for the Small—The Big Will Follow

There just aren't many big things in leadership. People who do not put forth the effort to provide day-to-day leadership because they are waiting for some large need to arise so that they can save the day are not leaders. You may have heard someone say, *"Just let me know when you want me to take care of that for you."* The speaker of this sentence will not provide quality leadership to anyone; he just wants to be the hero.

Just what are those small leadership actions? They are the visible things that people care about. Respecting and trying to accommodate peoples' more basic needs will encourage them to be respectful of and want to follow you.

One in three workers surveyed recently (per the *Los Angeles Times*) said they had accepted or quit a job because of basic working conditions. The workers' biggest complaint was hot-as-the-tropics heating or Antarctic air conditioning. The second most significant issue was workplace cleanliness, particularly the bathrooms. These do not seem like good reasons to jeopardize one third of a work force that is often expensive to replace!

Most complaints that employees have don't sound like big deals. They are little things that will lead to the big things. When you deal with the smaller issues that people care about, you build an environment of mutual respect that will result in the willingness to follow your lead.

Here's a tip on how to show people you respect their basic needs. If the air conditioner, or furnace, or toilet is not working, put up a small sign next to the offending thermostat or in the bathroom that reads, "We have called the repairman to fix this problem. I regret that you're inconvenienced while we all have to wait." Sign your name to the sign and, of course, do call the repairman. This small gesture shows that you are paying attention to and care about your employees' basic needs. It is respectful. It may also prevent you from having to hear over and over again, *Do you know that it's really hot in the conference room?"*

What sorts of little things resonate with others? Sometimes you just don't know what others care about. You may have to ask, and for sure, you'll want to watch and to listen! You will be able to identify the little things when you are being authentic with others and respectful to them. You will learn to be authentic and how to demonstrate true respect for others when you are listening to Life's Lessons.

Respect means recognizing that people are valuable and **giving people what they deserve, what they need, and what they want.**

One of the things that others **deserve** from you while you are leading them is your preparation time and effort. The basic fact that you should know what you're talking about with them, and prepare properly for meetings and/or dialogues, is a given. Not much additional explanation is required here. No real leader ever attempts (or is able to) "wing it" very often. When you hear someone say, *"I didn't have time to prepare,"* your likely (mostly to yourself) response may be, *"Then why do you think I want to take my time to listen?"* If you have honestly and uncharacteristically not had time to prepare, this is not the time to spew out the unvarnished truth. It's better to not say anything about your lack of preparation. Just be prepared to question for clarification and to listen carefully to the answers.

There is another aspect of preparing for and giving people what they deserve that is sometimes overlooked because it's also in the category of the little things. Most people want their leaders to look like leaders to them, and to others. People want and deserve your "professional presence." You may never hear this point called out specifically; however, you will hear it when people tell others about your leadership. You may hear comments like, *"Everybody knew that when Marcia walked into the meeting, she had it together."* You may hear people brag to others about the "killer" presentation you gave. These comments are affirmations that the time and effort you put into preparing yourself to look like a leader and preparing your materials to talk like a leader were well spent.

The most visible evidence of professional presence is the ability to stand up and present well. If there is one skill that a leader really has to perfect, it's the ability to give great presentations. Although it's not a completely comfortable situation for almost anyone, a leader has to present often and well to be credible and effective. Do not be concerned about being a little nervous when you have to present. If you aren't nervous, you shouldn't be standing up there. Not being at least a little nervous means that you aren't smart enough to know that it's really important to do well, and you are not respectful enough of your audience's time and attention to prepare well. Taking the time and expending the energy to prepare yourself to present well is not really about you. It means that you are being respectful of the time and intelligence of the people who are listening to you. It's about them. It's another little thing that will lead to bigger things.

Professional presence, by looking and dressing the part, also shows respect for others. This does not mean designer suits all the time! It means dressing professionally and appropriately, with subtle but visible signs that you took the time to look your best—for them.

I once chided a consultant colleague (who needs to remain nameless) for showing up at a client site without a tie. (The clients were wearing ties.) The consultant said that he thought that wearing a tie was "overrated." I didn't even understand what that meant! I think it really meant that he just didn't like wearing ties.

I offered this life lesson. *"If you are invited to dinner at someone's house, doesn't the first impression—what you see when you walk in— indicate how much regard the hosts have for you? If the house is super clean, the table is set beautifully, and maybe there are fresh flowers or little treats sitting around, you must be important to them. They took the time to prepare things as well as they could because you were coming. If you have to clear newspapers off the chair to sit down and the dining room table is still covered with their kids' homework projects, then you must not count for as much with them. They didn't even bother to fix things up for you."* I suggested that dressing professionally was the same thing. It is a sign that you respect the people with whom you're working because you've made an obvious effort to look good for them. (I'd like to say that my example made a difference to the consultant. Unfortunately, it did not. He was just too unwilling to inconvenience himself by ensuring more appropriate professional presence for others. On to Plan B with him: *"In spite of your belief about the relative importance of wearing a tie, you need to show up with one the next time you come here."*)

Share the Love

Another thing that people deserve from you as their leader is that you will share the credit for good things. Implying or outright stating that you did whatever wonderful thing is being talked about is dishonest, selfish, disrespectful, and really poor leadership. No leader accomplishes all good things alone! No good comes from grabbing the credit that should be given to or at least shared by others.

When I was in the field of private, post-secondary education, our school introduced a new degree program for Fashion Merchandising. Part of my responsibility was to help design and oversee the build-out of the physical space to house the new classes. It certainly needed to look different from our classrooms for Computer Science! We held a lavish school opening for the new program that was attended by all the executives of the company that owned the school (and several other schools as well). My staff of deans and I proudly conducted tours of the new facility for all of our corporate people, local politicians, news media, and 100 other invited guests.

Instead of signifying the classrooms with the customary "I, II, III" or "A, B, C," one of the deans (unfortunately I now forget which one) suggested naming them for fashion designers in alphabetic order. The classroom signs read "Armani, Balenciaga, Chanel, Dior," and so on. The president of our company was quite impressed with the signage and asked, *"Who came up with the naming idea for the rooms? Now, tell me the truth. Don't just say this was your idea."* I was so surprised at the question that I couldn't answer immediately. Why did he feel the need to add that I shouldn't take credit for this? While I pondered this for a few seconds, he continued with, *"All I ever hear at the other schools is 'I did this and this and this.'"*

What a sad commentary on the leadership skills (or lack thereof) that resided in our company. I felt bad for the president that he felt the need to head off another potential credit-grabber. Of course I intended to give the proper credit to the woman who owned the idea. Besides being the respectful thing to do, it was also a credit to me to have and to foster creative people in my own organization. There are all sorts of benefits from giving proper credit.

In addition to giving people what they deserve, also giving them what they **need and want** is a small indicator of respect that leads to large things.

We often don't realize the magnitude of the impact when we give others the small gift of respect and authenticity. You may not recognize right away the impact that those little things have on others. But when you find out about them—they can become a Life Lesson that you will want to listen to!

I am the oldest of five children: four girls and one "baby brother." Being the oldest meant that I did lots of babysitting growing up—way too much if you asked me then (or now). It seemed that there was always one to four siblings hanging on to me!

I must have had a homework assignment to write a poem when I was 16 years old, and I must have been babysitting (again) when I wrote it. I'm guessing that's what happened because I don't remember the exact circumstances. I only know that I came across this poem in a stack of old papers about 16 years later.

Little Sister

Now, listen, little sister,

All dressed for bed,

It's not the time

For tears to be shed.

You can't stay up

For all your crying

So stop that sniffling

And alibi-ing.

Now give me a kiss…

Oh, that's just fine. I love you too,

Little sister of mine.

Oh, such a big hug,

So warm and so sweet…

Well, maybe just an hour,

For a good girl's treat.

Jeanne E., Ursuline Academy, Feb. 19, '64

After I found the poem again, I had it engraved on plaques and gave one to each of my sisters for Christmas that year. There was much delight and lots of tears (Italian family!), and a question from each of them that I did not anticipate properly: *"Who did you write the poem for?"* Arrgghh...it could have been any of the three! But that was not, and still is not, an acceptable answer to any of them. Each sister wanted to be the "inspiration," the much-loved principal character in the poem. I could understand that—I just couldn't exactly remember! So, I told each of them privately, *"I wrote the poem for you."* I have had to repeat this statement to each of them during all family gatherings and on all birthday cards for the past almost 30 years—because they keep asking!

Sisters, here it is again.

"Pattie, I wrote the poem for you."

"Carol, I wrote the poem for you."

"Geri, I wrote the poem for you."

The truth is that I probably wrote the poem for all of them. It was just easier to use a singular "sister" word than a plural "sisters." I never anticipated that the recognition, the respect, and the love shown by a poem written by a 16-year-old would have such an impact. I'm glad that it did. I'm also glad for the chance to re-affirm the Life Lesson about authenticity and respect every time I hear the question, *"Who did you write the poem for?"* The question reminds me often that doing the little things for others respectfully and authentically can reap benefits for all parties for a lifetime.

There is no time limit on showing respect for others and authenticity toward them. Even if you don't actually see the outcomes immediately, or even not ever, the value is still there. Being authentic with and respectful to others builds the foundation for the "deliver-ables" of providing quality leadership—making things happen and getting what you want.

CHAPTER 10

Get What You Want...or Change What You Want

*Leaders provide **comfort and calm** to others in times of change or ambiguity so that others can be accepting of the changes around them.*

LEADERSHIP IS ALL about effecting change—in processes, ways of acting, thinking, doing business, attitudes, or environment. Leading people to change acceptance is such an enormous topic for leaders that exploring the entire arena is actually another entire book. For the purpose of providing guidance in "walking the change talk," however, you'll see some highlights on how to make it happen in this chapter.

As a leader, getting what you want means being able to get others to accept and work toward achieving the objectives of your change initiatives. In times of change, all people need the **Four Cs of Change: Comfort, Competence, Confidence, and Control.** These are the elements that people require in order to accept, embrace, and fully realize the benefits of current and anticipated changes. As their leader, it is both your responsibility and your privilege to lead your people gently, but firmly, into the "promised land" of your planned changes by ensuring that they have the 4 Cs.

Initiatives that drive necessary changes rarely fail because change wasn't needed or was poorly planned or poorly executed. They fail because of the natural resistance that accompanies all changes—regardless of the magnitude of the changes.

People are familiar and comfortable with "the way things are." Even if the current state of things is difficult or time-consuming, or produces less than the desired outcomes—and even if your followers know that—they may still cling to the known ways like they were life preservers on a sinking ship. People may recognize rationally that a change needs to be made, but will they be able to easily accept it on an emotional level? Likely not. Remember this? *"It may be a three-legged, diseased dog with one-ear, but it's* **my** *dog!"*

Accepting change is not all reason and logic. Acceptance or resistance is rooted in visceral, emotional responses. Resistance starts with "how I feel" about something, and then, as the 4 Cs are being achieved, moves to "how I think" about something. Changes in process, the way people do their jobs, could cause people concern about their own jobs, or their value to the company, or even not being able to ride to work in the car pool they've been in for seven years.

Part of the emotionality of the situation comes from the implicit message in changes you may be trying to bring about. Because processes, approaches, ways of doing business, and attitudes need to be changed, it must mean that they were wrong in the first place...and therefore the people doing/possessing them were wrong. This is the covert perception that people often have. No one likes to hear or think they might be wrong!

For any change to be successful, the people who are impacted by it must be willing and able to accept and benefit from the change. To be willing to accept change, people must feel comfortable and have confidence in your leadership. To be able to benefit from change, they must feel competent and confident in themselves, and in control. This reality increases the requirement for you, as their leader, to possess comfort, competence, confidence, and control. You are the one at the head of the pack. You are the "face of change." The way you lead is the way people will follow!

Just how can you provide comfort and calm to your followers in times of change? It begins with feeling that way yourself. But what if you don't? What if the change is also hard for you? Then lie to yourself! If you tell yourself often enough, *"I am comfortable and confident that this will be successful,"* you will likely begin to believe it yourself! In the meantime, while you're waiting to find real comfort and calm yourself, you'll be projecting the attitude that your followers need.

When You Need to Make Change Happen

While you're convincing yourself, you also need to accept that others may have a difficult time with or lengthy adjustment period to whatever change you're leading. There are two different, but equally bad, attitudes that (unsuccessful) leaders take toward others' acceptance of their initiatives: The Firing Squad and the Field of Dreams.

The Firing Squad school of thought on effecting change in a business environment is, *"They don't have a choice. They change or they're out. Line 'em up against the wall and shoot 'em. It's going to happen."* (Sorry men—but here I go again defaming you. This is a particularly male attitude towards the change challenge.) From my almost twenty years of experience in supporting projects for business process improvement and integrated information systems implementations, I know that's not true. People don't have to change. There are an impressive (read: disastrous) number of ways that people can derail what could be a successful initiative that would result in much-needed changes.

Another less-than-successful approach is the Field of Dreams. Just because you've conceived of it and built it, they will come. No, they won't. It's **your** concept and **your** dream. It's not yet theirs. People need to see, feel, and accept the wisdom and value in what you're proposing before they'll show up to play on your team in your field of dreams. They need to know why they should show up and play. What's in it for them?

I once had a foolish neighbor whose life's goal consisted primarily of being rich. I asked him how he planned to achieve his goal, and he said he entered lots of contests and had sent in 10 entries to the Publishers Clearing House Sweepstakes. I believe my neighbor was expecting Ed McMahon to knock on his door any day with that over-sized check! That field of dreams was probably not going to appear. It's the same type of delusion that makes some leaders believe that just because they want it to, it will happen. Just wanting and believing does not make it so!

When you think and feel from their perspective, when you understand and empathize with their need to have the 4 Cs, you will have the words and the tools to provide the comfort and the calm your people need. (You may want to review Chapter 6 about finding the right words now. I'll wait for you to come back.)

The need to be comfortable and calm and to provide that same type of solace to your followers may be fairly easy to understand and accept. But what about the part of, "If you don't get what you want, change what you want"? Does this title imply that you should waver on your own commitment and goals? No. It means that you will recognize that sometimes your mission's scope, your process, and/or your approach may not quite fit the bill. They just may not contribute to your getting the job done, which is getting what you want. A prudent attitude in this situation is to remain flexible and change the things that you can and should in order to achieve what you do *not* want changed, which is the successful result you're striving for.

Sometimes, you have to change what you want because of the following:

- ► You shouldn't have asked for it in the first place
- ► New information or requirements appear
- ► The harsh light of reality tells you that it's just not going to happen

What Life Lesson illustrates that sometimes you just **shouldn't have asked for it in the first place?**

Life Lesson #12: Did I Hear You Right?

Many years ago, I decided I wanted to be a home builder. The fact that I knew almost nothing about blueprints, lumber, power tools, or cement did not deter me. I aggressively pursued and got a job as a sales person in a large building center in northern Minnesota.

After I had been on the job for three months, I discovered that I was hired primarily because they needed to hire a woman. The company was a large chain of building centers (that needs to remain nameless) with over 600 sales MEN...no women. The U.S. Equal Employment Opportunity Commission was on their backs. I was as unhappy to learn that I was hired because of gender as I would have been to learn that I was denied for the same reason. Okay, I would just make sure that the company learned that gender had nothing to do with success in their testosterone-heavy industry! By the second year, I was the top sales PERSON in the company.

At the building center, our job was to sell anything possibly related to building and remodeling either as stand-alone items for do-it-yourselfers or as packages for home builders. Selling a home package started with reading the blueprints and creating the materials list for the structure being built. I had so much to learn, but I had a whole herd of construction people (customers!) to teach me. (My work colleagues weren't too keen on helping me learn for the first year because I was "built wrong" for the construction business. Oh well. I had customers to teach me. Besides, I knew my co-workers would come around when they saw it was to their advantage to work with me instead of against me. They eventually figured it out, and they changed their tune.)

During a late shift on a slow, snowy, winter's night, I was working the sales counter with another colleague when a man entered carrying a package. He immediately went to my male counterpart for help. I was glad of that. I could tell by the package that he was coming in with a problem. I was not in the mood to solve small do-it-yourself problems that night. This was the conversation I overheard.

Customer: *"I wanna return this shower head."*
Sales Guy: *"Sure. What's the problem? Doesn't it work?"*
Customer: *"Don't know."*

With a quizzical look, the Sales Guy asked, *"Then why do you want to return it?"*
Customer: *"I don't need no shower head."*
Sales Guy: *"Oh, okay. Does the one you have work all right for you?"*
Customer: *"Don't have no shower head."*

Now the Sales Guy was really perplexed.

Sales Guy: *"Then why wouldn't you need this shower head?"*
Customer: *"Because I don't have no shower."*

"I don't have no shower, but I bought a shower head." Could I have heard that right! I struggled hard to keep from laughing out loud,

but my eyes kept filling with tears from the effort. Thankfully, the customer and the Sales Guy were just staring at each other for a few minutes while the Sales Guy was "processing" the information. Sales Guy obviously did not know how to respond and eventually just turned and walked away! I regained my composure (almost), stepped in, and sold the customer a shower. Clearly, the customer just needed to change what he wanted! He had obviously wanted the wrong thing in the first place!

Some months later, I was again working the sales counter during a busy, Saturday morning. The store was filled with contractors and homeowners milling around the counter, waiting to place orders for their materials. They were all men, except for one woman who was standing off to the side, away from the carpenter crowd. She was obviously out of her element. She had a small list gripped tightly with both hands, and her eyes were screaming, *"What am I doing here?"* I motioned for the woman to approach the counter, and she stepped up with obvious relief on her face. She was immediately more comfortable because a woman was going to help her. She wouldn't have to worry about looking foolish to one of the men. The woman figured that I would understand, and she was right. I certainly knew what it felt like to be the "odd (wo)man out."

This was our exchange. (To appreciate the conversation, whenever you read "x", say to yourself the letter X—do not say "by.")

Jeanne: *"Can I help you?"*
Shopping Woman: *"Yes, I'd like to buy some wood. I have the list that my husband wrote up."*
Jeanne: *"Sure, what do you need?"*
Shopping Woman: *"First, I'd like 8 pieces that are 2 x 6 x 12."*

Short pause, while I wondered if I should tell her that "x" is actually said "by." No, that will only make her feel like she did something wrong. It sure won't help her anxiety level.

Jeanne: "Okay. What else?"

Shopping Woman: "I'd like 36 pieces that are 1 x 10 x 10, and 20 pieces that are 1 x 6 x 10, and I need 50 pieces that are 2 x 4."

Something was missing.

Jeanne: "How long would you like those 2 x 4's?" (I said the letter X and not "by.")

The woman hesitated briefly and then said, "Oh, we don't need them for very long. We're just building a lean-to."

I was afraid to speak for a few seconds because I knew I would start laughing—not a good thing to do.

Finally, I said, "I'm sorry. I asked that question wrong. I meant to say how long would you like those pieces of 2 x 4 to be? Should they be 8 feet long, or 12 feet, or some other length?"

The woman put her head down, moved closer to me, and said in a whisper, "That was really dumb, wasn't it?"

Jeanne (hesitating): "Yes, but I have heard dumber. How about if I give you 8 foot lengths? That's what your husband probably wants. And, when you go out to the yard to pick these up, if you say lumber instead of pieces of wood, and if you say "by" whenever you see an X, then all the guys out there are going to figure that you're the one doing the building. They'll be way impressed!"

The woman gave me a co-conspirator's grin, paid for her pieces of wood, and confidently marched out to the yard to get her...lumber.

My shower-less customer and the woman who was only building a lean-to provided another valuable Life Lesson: *Sometimes what you want is too much, too soon, too large, or just the wrong thing...or you didn't really understand what you were asking for. Get what you want...or change what you want and then get it.*

Get It or Change It

The speed bumps in your success path may have appeared simply because other people didn't have the confidence or comfort to accept the impact or the timing of the change. Or, maybe it really is too much and too fast for them. Maybe it's just not the right thing to do and you didn't fully recognize that the outcome wasn't a good one when you originally defined your desired results. If you discover that the outcome has missed its intended mark, then modify what you want to the right degree of change and the timing that is reasonable and acceptable... and to the correct result. You have a right to change your mind!

This is not a gender-specific right. Men can and do change their minds, although probably not as often as women appear to. Women hear more often than men, *"Why don't you just make up your mind?"* Men may be mind-changing averse because they perceive that changing is a sign of weakness. Maybe sometimes it is, but sometimes it's just smart and prudent. Mind-changing has a bad reputation. If, when you receive better information and have determined that what you wanted doesn't fit what should happen, then false pride is prompting the tight grip on the original decision. It's the weak people who do not change their decisions when they learn more about what or how something should be. It's the unwise who make up their minds in the first place without sufficient information.

It's amazing to me how the media attacks politicians for flip-flopping on an issue. *"Senator, seven years ago you voted against this bill, and now you're expressing support. You've flip-flopped on your decision."* The Senator then spends way too much time during several ensuing interviews explaining that his previous "no" and today's "yes" are really the same thing. Seldom do we ever believe his protestations that he has *"always stayed the course."* But, why should he? How hard is it to say this:

> *"Seven years ago, I didn't have the information that I have now. What appeared to be a good thing then for our country is no longer good. That's why I changed my support. I won't hold onto a bad position in the face of today's information and situation."* It doesn't seem like it would be so hard to be forthright and honest—but it must be. I don't hear those politicians saying that. But if I did—that one would get my vote!

If the concept of sometimes getting what you want by changing what you want is still a little hazy, this quote from Confucius may help clarify it for you. *"When it is obvious that the goals cannot be reached, don't adjust the goals, adjust the action steps."* Don't lose (read: change) the vision—you may just have to change the way you get there!

Tell the Others Why

The key to getting what you want on the second round (when you have changed your mind about the action steps) is to communicate to your followers that the objective is changing slightly and/or the approach or timing is being altered. You do not have to say that you were wrong with your first plan (leadership is not a confessional); nor do you have to punish yourself every time you need to modify your original plans. Remember, you have a right to change your mind! The "rule" for communicating a change because what you wanted was too much, too soon, or wrong is to simply broadcast the information about the changes in the strategy or the timelines and then seek support on the new and improved approach. (Yes, there are exceptions to this rule. But you have to start with a rule or you can't recognize an exception.)

Occasionally (actually, quite often if you work in a fast-paced, dynamic environment), **new information or requirements develop** that necessitate a change in the outcome, which means you may need to alter your objectives or your approach or both. You may have been charged with developing and rolling out new HR processes for your retail chain company to make the hiring and on-boarding processes more efficient. You need to be able to accomplish more in less time because your company is expanding rapidly and your industry has a high turnover rate. You are making progress on your plans to re-vamp processes when your company's executives announce that they are closing one third of the stores because of an overall economic down-turn. This means that a large number of people will now be laid off, both in the field and at the corporate level. You still need to revamp your processes, but now the reason why has changed. Your challenge with the new information and requirements is to be able to handle the impact of all the imminent layoffs efficiently, effectively, and em-pathetically.

The change in situation requires a different approach and time-line and certainly a change in the messaging to your followers. The key to the right communication in this situation is to be proactive (before they hear too many of the rumors through the grapevine!), calming, and comforting, and to be honest about the company's plans to the extent that you've been authorized to reveal. If you do not agree with the company's decision, this is not the time to share your angst. If you can't be authentic and honest when publicly supporting the decision at first—at the least, don't criticize it! Your followers don't need to hear that you are against what you will be leading them toward. It's not good for them or for the ultimate outcome that you need to achieve...and it's certainly not good for your own career path if your supervisors find out that you've "bad mouthed" the corporate deci-sion! Just change what you want...and then get what you want!

Another reason you may have to change what you want is that you can finally tell that **it's just not going to happen.** You have done everything you can to achieve your objectives as you've identified and understood them. You have communicated effectively and led consistently and with clarity of direction. You've faced all the risks and challenges and have instituted all the mitigating and resolution processes that you knew were needed and that were under your control. But, even still, the desired end result is just not going to happen. Now what? Now it's time to re-examine your actions, objectively and dispassionately. (Even better, ask your mentor to help you examine them. You may have a problem with the objective part on your own. I remember, with pain, thinking that I had done "everything right," only to hear my mentor ask, *"Just what were you thinking? Bad Jeanne!"*)

If what you want is still the right thing at the right time, but it's not going to happen because of your leadership actions, then don't keep doing what you've been doing. Albert Einstein is credited with this definition of insanity: *Insanity is doing the same thing over and over again and expecting different results.* You have the right to change! Besides the change-right, you want to remember that no one is really "precious." Sometimes we have to say, *"I'm sorry."* It's not going to kill us.

There are other reasons why it may be time to change what you want or how you want to get it. If you believe that you have **really** done everything you can to lead effectively toward change and the change still isn't coming to fruition, then it's possible that your plans, process, or objectives contained elements that are just not under your immediate control. An example is that you may have needed the agreement or support of someone (a C-level person perhaps, or someone from another department or office) to whom you don't have access. This scenario often occurs when you are working on changes that will have an ancillary impact on others. One of the tenets of negotiation is that you can't reach agreement with someone "who isn't in the room." If the necessary person isn't part of the communication and planning (either by design or accessibility), then you may not have her vital agreement and support when you need it.

If you need the support of someone to whom you do not currently have access, then it may be time to either change your objective or change your process of leading. You may need to find the right person and/or communication path to lead you to your required supporter. If/when you do get to that person, you may then need to change a part of your objectives also. If that person really is significant to your success and has previously been "blocking" or ignoring your work, there might be a reason that you need to hear! It's time to listen and accommodate or incorporate what you'll hear into your process or objectives. It's time to change what you want...then to get what you want.

Taking Care of Others in Times of Change

While you're getting what you want—the realization of your vision—it's important to remember that when you change your mind or your direction you are also changing the direction of the people you are leading. They may need some "adjustment time."

The willingness and ability to provide comfort and calm to your followers in times of change is one of the characteristics and requirements of being a superior leader. Actually making those changes happen is one of the activities and responsibilities that a leader has to accept. Just what do you need to do to effect the changes you're leading? The following six steps summarize the Leading for Change process:

1. Identify what needs to be changed and the extent of the change required

2. Don't ignore or discount the reality that others will not immediately embrace the vision or willingly support it

3. Communicate the need for change in a way that will encourage others to share your vision and accept the need

4. Determine how your people feel about the impending change

5. Provide the support your people need to ensure they can and will participate appropriately and "give you what you want"

6. Celebrate publicly the small victories on your path to change and mourn in private over the defeats

After following the Leading for Change steps, if you don't "get what you want"..."change what you want" and try the steps again.

A more in-depth look at the steps will provide some additional information on why and how to provide effective change leadership.

Step 1: I assume that you are able and willing to **identify the need** or you wouldn't have begun the initiative. The second part of this step is **to recognize the difference** between the way things are now and how they will be after your change initiative is completed, and to know who will be impacted. If your entire nursing department will change the way the inventory carts on the floors are being re-stocked, the change could have an impact on purchasing, shipping, and receiving departments, along with the warehouse. The change could also involve the finance department if the recognition of expenses will be changed as a result of the change in the re-stocking procedure. This large-impact type of situation requires a different type of change leadership with a broader "reach" than if your initiative is to change from a fundraising dinner dance to a golf tournament for your favorite charity.

Having a clear understanding of the resultant impact of your plans is the key to successful execution and to knowing that you actually did achieve the right goals. Yogi Berra said it clearly (or as clearly as he ever said anything) when he advised us that, *"If you don't know where you are going, you might end up someplace else."*

Step 2: Recognizing that **others may not immediately embrace your vision** is a step that needs its own place in the process of effecting change. If this step is not called out separately, it can easily be overlooked and may not even be included in the change planning process. Overlooking this possibility (read: probability) that others will not immediately embrace your vision is called the "ostrich approach." Even though those big birds don't really stick their heads in the sand, they are so "heads down" that they can't see what's going on around them. It's definitely more prudent to call out resistance as a potential risk to your success and to make plans to mitigate that risk early in your planning. As a reminder, the Firing Squad and Field of Dreams approaches are not recommended mitigation strategies!

If there is immediate and overwhelming change acceptance to your initiative, you can save your strategy as the starter for the next change initiative you lead. If you never experience any resistance to your plans, however, you may be setting your leadership sights too low! An insight to the presence of resistance in change is provided by Wes Roberts, PhD., in his book *Leadership Secrets of Attila the Hun.*[11] Dr. Roberts tell us: *"Always remember that worthy causes meet with the most resistance—even internal withholding of support and loyalty. If victory is easily gained, you must reconsider the worthiness of your ambitions."*

Even small changes that you may believe are no-brainers may not be immediately embraced. I remember vividly the first time I tried to institute a dress code for weekend work on campus at a private college in Texas. There wasn't a real dress code for Saturdays and Sundays and most of the staff seemed to favor shorts or sweats and beer-logo

---

[11] Wes Roberts, Ph.D. *Leadership Secrets of Attila the Hun* (Warner Books, 1989).

t-shirts. At that time, I was so naïve that I thought a weekend dress code would be an easy request. People just needed to know why it was important. I explained that I certainly appreciated their willingness to work on the weekends periodically. The challenge was that we had a large number of potential students with their parents who toured the campus on Saturdays, and the image we portrayed with the too-casual (read: sloppy and ugly) attire was not consistent with the standards of our school. The students' dress code at the time was business dress: ties for the men and nylons and business pumps for the women. I asked for business casual dress on Saturdays in keeping with our school values.

Almost immediately after sending out the mass communication about the weekend dress code for the staff, the "buzz" was audible. The few teachers who always looked professional appeared in my office doorway to make sure that their clothing was appropriate. The rest of the staff, including those who sometimes looked like they had come to work just after washing their cars, did not appear to be concerned at all. What followed was three weeks of talking, talking, talking. I never knew how many questions people could ask about the exact meaning of "business casual." I finally brought in catalogues and Sunday paper department store ads with pictures of business casual outfits circled. I knew that people knew what I meant by "business casual." They just didn't want to do it!

I never again approached a dress code change or enforcement with such a cavalier, naïve attitude. I had learned my lesson. Even what I believe is a small change may be a much bigger deal to others. They just might not be eager to jump on my bandwagon or "share my vision."

Step 3: You would think it would be fairly easy to **communicate the need for change.** The challenge is that too often we are singing the wrong song for our audience.

There are many mission statements for change initiatives that read something like this: *"We are undertaking this significant project to lower our cost of doing business in order to increase the profitability we need to continue to grow our company in a dynamic, competitive marketplace."* Okay...so what?

Does the AP clerk or anyone else (besides the person who wrote this mission statement) understand what the statement means to them? Probably not. We all read and interpret messages from our own perspectives. We are personally vested in our careers. We eagerly devote our time, energy, and talents to the betterment of our companies...and ourselves. We read a mission statement like this and think, *"So, what does that platitudinous pile of words mean to me? Why should I care? Why should I have to change what I've been doing—which, by the way, has been effective, thank you very much!"*

People need to hear change messages from their perspective. When you've prepared an announcement about your initiative, read it aloud to yourself, but listen to it with your followers' ears. Think from their perspective. What will they care about? What will their concerns be? You will want to provide personal, authentic reasons or desired outcomes that your people can relate to and accept. A mission statement or call for support doesn't have to be difficult or complex to be good. Simple, straightforward, easy-to-relate-to messaging is good.

Step 4: Determine how your people feel about the impending change by watching, listening to, and asking them. Even better, get someone else to ask them. Since you are the "face of the change," people may be reluctant to be totally forthright in how they feel. They may not want to appear disloyal to you or the company. They might be concerned about being perceived as complainers. They may even be unsure about how they feel and need to process verbally or to vent.

Try to identify a change agent who can help you determine how the others feel about the upcoming change. The best change agent for you is someone who is positive and enthusiastic in addition to being widely accepted by others in the organization. Also, being in support of your vision is a must! The change agent can support your initiative by being another set of eyes and ears for you.

Warning! I am not encouraging you to set up a "spy ring." This is not a covert operation. You and your change agent should make it clear that you want to hear your people's honest, gut-level feeling about the initiative's objectives and plans so you can then provide the right amount and level of support for them.

If your initiative includes substantive change or has implications across multiple areas of your organization, you should consider contracting support from an outside firm that specializes in managing change. Examples of these types of initiatives are business process redesigns (lots of them, not just one process), changing the information system to another package, downsizing with a number of imminent layoffs, or integrating a newly purchased company into your organization. As the degree of change increases, so do the risks. The greater the change the greater the need to seek qualified support in order to mitigate timeline delays or failure because of change resistance.

It is difficult to move to Step 5 and provide support to your followers in times of change when you aren't really sure about what type of support they need. What are their concerns? The list of reasons why people are resistant to change includes the following:

► They believe their needs are being met already

► They believe the change will make it harder for them to meet their needs

► They believe the costs outweigh the benefits

► They believe the change process is being handled improperly

► They believe the change will fail

► They believe the change is inconsistent with their values

► They believe those responsible for the change cannot be trusted

You'll want to do whatever is required to determine how to help your people help you. This situation is all about getting what you want...and you want a successful change initiative. Ask, listen, and learn. Enlist change agents to help support you. Know when it's time to seek outside support, and then listen to and learn from that support. When you know why, then you can determine what, how, and when.

Step 5: Provide the support your people need to understand, accept, and support your initiative. There is a misconception in change leadership that the only action needed to effect change acceptance is communication. Too often the words "change management" and "communication" are used synonymously. They are not, however, interchangeable. They are not the same thing. Communication about the goals, the plans, the timelines, and the successes (or hiccoughs) is a *supporting action* for change management. Communication that is clear, timely, honest, and audience-focused is a necessary activity in most initiatives, but it is not the end-all, be-all for providing change leadership.

Knowing what other types of support you need to provide to your followers, in addition to quality communication, depends on the results of your listening to their concerns (Step 4). As I mentioned in the beginning of this chapter, the entire discussion of leading to effect change is fodder for a whole other book; however, here are some examples of additional supporting actions to provide superior leadership in effecting change:

▶ Visible signs of the project and the change illustrate that the project is really going to happen. These signs of change include naming the project, selecting a symbol or graphic that will provide a visual reminder of the project, and/or setting up information tents on the tables in the lunch rooms or on company bulletin boards. Too many people discount the importance of naming a significant change initiative. It really is like letting your kids name the stray dog. Once it has a name—you just can't get rid of it! The name should be something that is symbolic of what the initiative represents—something people can relate to. It's not likely that your kids will call the stray mutt "Dog." In turn, you don't want to call your plans "New HR Processes." It's time to let those creative juices flow!

▶ An intranet with a Frequently Asked Questions site where people impacted by your initiative can post their questions and concerns can be an effective communication tool.

Caution—someone actually has to answer the postings. If you can't be certain that this will happen, then don't create the site. Providing a way for people to ask questions but then never answering the questions will be counterproductive to your successful change leadership!

▶ Requests for their input on meeting and training schedules helps others feel more in control and less "managed." Give your people choices—after making sure that all the choices will work with your plans and timelines. Asking instead of telling raises the acceptance level of a change exponentially!

► Short, frequent communications that highlight accomplishments of individuals who are working with you on the project area a great way to boost morale during a change. Interview an "end user" or someone else who will be impacted by the initiative, and broadcast their feelings and thoughts about the project. Change is easier for people to accept when the messaging is coming from one of their own.

► Formal training in professional skills, such as team building, conflict resolution, problem solving...or other skills your people need to feel competent in doing whatever it is you want them to do, will help them develop all 4 Cs of change.

► Your attendance at other department meetings to answer questions about the changes or project, if your project has cross-over impact, will bolster communication between all parties affected by the change.

If what you are doing doesn't seem to be working well, then change what you're doing as often as you need to...until you get what you want! Recognize that a valid approach that is not working well is an indicator of continuing resistance that needs to be changed to acceptance. Signs of resistance include hearing the following:

► *"I'm (or my people are) too busy to attend that team meeting (or that class.) Exactly when are you going to be covering XXX topic. I can come in for 15 minutes to hear that part.*" We always seem to find time for the things we care about and support. If we don't want something, we don't have time.

▶ *"Tell me again why we're doing this?"* If you've heard this question more than two times from the same person, it's not confusion—it's resistance.

▶ *"I think we need to revisit the plans and the timing again."* If you've already received a group's approval and acceptance and you're hearing this for the third time, they need more change leadership from you—not more revisiting of the plans.

▶ *"I was talking to my friend in another company, and she said that they did this same thing and it was a disaster."* This person is telling you that she's afraid of failure. She needs some comfort and calming from her leader.

People need to feel and believe that they will be successful in their efforts. A strong leader first identifies the impediments to her people's success. She then removes the roadblocks by providing the support her followers need to understand, accept, and support the changes.

Step 6: Celebrate publicly the small victories and mourn in private over the defeats. It's unusual for every plan to go exactly as you planned it. Getting what you want often means a few steps forward, stumbling a little, recovering, inching forward again, getting spun around, recovering...again and again. Almost every day, a leader has some triumphs and some defeats. (It's a given that you want to work toward keeping the ratio of victories over defeats high!) In most lifetimes, there are not a large number of really big triumphs to celebrate. If you wait for monumental events, you may not see and won't be able to share the joy of the small ones. Everyone needs the "rush" of celebration to help get them through the stumbling, minor defeat periods—even you, the leader!

> My husband and I used to keep a bottle of nice (read: too expensive) champagne at the ready to celebrate the small good things in life. It was a great idea for awhile. The problem was that I'm well practiced at reaching for and seeing a silver lining in the storm clouds. I had conditioned myself to look for and rejoice in the small victories because I knew I needed to build my emotional reserves to get past the defeats. That translated to lots of celebrations and too much champagne! After some time, champagne was getting to be a standard line item on our monthly budget and the sound of popping corks was just too frequent for stable, "civilized" people. My husband and I decided to eliminate the champagne part of the celebration plan, although we've continued with the celebrations by talking about and rejoicing in whatever good happens every day.

As a leader, you want to provide those same small celebratory opportunities for your followers. Your people need to see and to share in your delight when small, good things happen. Celebrations can include a surprise delivery of cupcakes, a card that you post reading—*"You're too fine!"* or a periodic walk through their office area to say, *"You helped us get this far...and I'm so glad you did!"* Celebrate publicly! You don't get what you want by yourself. Share the excitement!

Mourning? That is different. While you certainly want to be upfront and honest about needing to re-tool, re-think, or recover from a setback, you don't want your followers to hear about or see your "keening" over what was lost. It is not good to vent publicly about *"the idiot in Purchasing who didn't do what he was supposed to"* or the fact that you've *"lost three weeks in getting this done because the bureaucrats can't think themselves out of a paper bag!"* This type of mourning is best done in the privacy of your linen closet at home. It is true that excising your negative thoughts by stomping about and agonizing may make you feel better immediately afterwards. (It certainly works for me!) However, sharing these moments is not productive for the people who look to you for leadership. They may not realize that it's just a part of your process for recovery. They may believe that "all is lost." If they do…then they are probably right. All may be lost, because they may not want to continue to follow you!

Leading others means that you get what you want. You work toward providing comfort and calm to others while you're getting what you want. If you're not getting what you want, then you have the right and the responsibility to change your mind and what you want. **Then,** get what you want!

CHAPTER 11

Walk Tall!

*Leaders inspire others to be **confident** of their direction and also help build the followers' personal confidence.*

NSPIRING CONFIDENCE IN others—this is a case of "you must have it to give it." If you can't build, sustain, and repeatedly re-build sincere confidence in yourself, it's doubtful that you can inspire or infuse confidence in others. Another challenge of the confidence requirement is that of all the characteristics of a leader, confidence is one of the most difficult to fake for long periods of time. People have a way of knowing when you are not "ringing true." If others see a false façade of "*I am confident in my ability to lead this team/initiative/party,*" they will question not only your capability and desirability as a leader, but also, they will question themselves. "*Can I really do this? Am I going to get the guidance and support I need? Hmmm...maybe I should just hold back for awhile and see if this is going anywhere.*" To lead effectively, you must have confidence and successfully demonstrate it. When you feel it and others see it, you are well positioned to lead effectively and successfully. Without it...not so much.

Faux leaders often display bravado and believe that they are exuding confidence. There is a fine line between confidence and arrogance. The line has been crossed onto the side of arrogance when a supposed leader has to tell others that she really is good at what she does. When, close in time, you hear tales of the same accomplishments repeated more than twice, what you are hearing is, *"Look at me! I'm really wonderful! I have accomplished so much more than anyone else."* If leaders have to say it themselves …they aren't that good. (An exception to this rule is political leaders. They need to repeat the same achievements and laud their own superior characteristics over and over again. We all seem to take a "so-what-have-you-done-for-me-today" approach with our political leaders. They need to remind us often of their accomplishments, as well as their own value, I suspect.)

It's the old-money, new-money difference. A faux leader wears "confidence" publicly and loudly, like the too-much gold jewelry on new-money people. Real leaders don't have to personally advertise their worth. The way they conduct themselves and the true relationships they build with others lets you know they are old-money leaders. They have less visible glitter—but you just know their jewelry cases at home are chock full of gold and diamonds!

What happens when we hear about or come across one of those faux leaders who are more flash than substance? We seem compelled to offer an instant and consistent excuse for an overbearing, arrogant, dictatorial person. *"She (he) must be suffering from low self-esteem."* This explanation is often offered immediately after someone else has reported that said person *"acts like he (she) is the second coming of Christ!"* Why do we automatically assume that the person has low self-esteem? Do we need to supply some sympathetic (she-is-suffering-so-that's-why she-acts-that-way) spin to someone else's bad behavior? Is it possible that we are trying to figure out how to accommodate or tolerate unacceptable behavior? Do we think we can "save" the person? Yes, sometimes we believe and are trying to do all of the above. It's the nurturing, caring part of being a woman that is, in almost all situations, one of the most desirable aspects of femininity. But sometimes, we carry it too far for too long. We try to nurture some people who don't really need or deserve it. What they need and deserve is a swift kick in the butt.

Maybe we're just being too nice. I'm not sure why we so readily suggest that an arrogant, over-bearing person suffers from some malady that will require us to make concessions for their suffering. Maybe they do have low self-esteem...and maybe they don't. It's possible that those in-your-face people really do have too **much** self-esteem. They could believe that they have nothing to learn because they already know everything twice. Maybe they're in the death grip of the Precious Devil! (See Chapter 4.)

I'm not suggesting that we shouldn't look after our colleagues who really do need to have their own confidence built up. The difference between our instant reactions of "kindness" and "prudent watchfulness" is a factor when the person in question is a leader, or pretends to be our leader. I am suggesting that none of us should have to accept, tolerate, or automatically follow leaders who are arrogant and overbearing. If you have any choice at all, don't follow the person, don't encourage others to do so, and for sure, don't let the person in question be you! You are and want to be a real, quality leader. That means confidence, not arrogance.

Even though most of the signs of confidence are small and subtle, we can instantly recognize truly confident leaders. We know them at a glance. We absorb very quickly their straight-shouldered but still comfortable posture, their head-up, look-us-in-the-eyes conversational style, and their "quiet" hands that aren't fidgeting or clenched in a death grip. We are drawn to the person whose body language says, *"Listen to me. I have something to say that you'll want to hear."* We can see this composure in others, and we can even consciously adopt the poses ourselves for those short periods when we have to "fake it until we make it." What is harder for us is to be forced to project confidence for more than say, 30 minutes, when we don't really feel it. When we have to keep thinking about looking confident, it's a sign that we need to re-build our real personal strength. Then we don't have to think about looking like it—we'll just have it and do it.

Another difficult aspect of appearing confident to others is knowing when we are doing it wrong or right. To find that out, we often have to listen to others. You've already been introduced to Paul Robson, our CIBER VP. One of Paul's well-honed skills is presentation. Even in difficult (read: potentially combative) situations and even when he's speaking extemporaneously, he's really good! (Since I've taught presentation skills for 15 years, you can trust this evaluation. I do know what "really good" is!) Paul is so well conditioned that, although he's appropriately nervous about standing up in front of a not-always-totally-receptive audience, he doesn't let them "see him sweat." However, he does make one small gesture that can expose his inner terror. Paul crosses his arms over his chest in an obvious "hiding," protectionism stance. He doesn't even realize that he starts his presentations that way almost every time. But he does listen with his ears and eyes. Before he begins speaking, Paul always (correctly) scans the room to connect with his audience. At that point, if any of "his" people cross and uncross their arms, Paul will immediately listen to the signal and drop his hands to his sides, where they belong. (Being highly "coach-able" is another of Paul's skills.)

We have to know when we're doing it wrong, and we have to know when we're showing true confidence. Whatever we did when we were right, we want to be able to gauge the impact of that confidence stance and remember it for the next, similar occasion. Another benefit of recognizing when we are appropriately demonstrating personal strength and conviction is that we can use those moments to shore up our own confidence. There are many confidence-lowering opportunities in a day's time. We want to balance the scorecard by tracking the good times also! Just like knowing when we are wrong, we know when we are appropriately demonstrating confidence and when it's beneficial to our leadership goals by listening to others.

When I returned to college as a non-traditional student (read: old) at the age of 35, my declared majors were Biology and Chemistry. I believe I was really majoring in "Partial Credit" because that was primarily my focus—getting more points for an almost-right answer on the tests. I was often in my professors' offices or on the phone with them pointing out just how close I was to the right answers. When I saw my Organic Chemistry professor walking down the hall right after distributing our graded test papers, I was delighted. I could never catch him in person. (All of my previous pleadings had been done by phone.) I went up to him quickly to get my grade changed before it was written in permanent ink in his grade book. His first words were, "*Wow, you're really short! From a distance, I thought you were 6' tall!*" Having heard this from people too often before, and having been annoyed by it every time, I'm sure a flash of irritation crossed my face. I thought, "*I know I'm short. I've been short all my life. Do you think I was 6' tall yesterday and I suddenly shrunk to 5'1'? Don't tell me I'm short—just change my grade!*"

Through the noise of my inner rebuttal, I heard the professor say, "*You probably want more points again, don't you? You're probably right. How many do you want?*" That's when I realized that my professor wasn't insulting me with the "*Wow, you're short*" remark—he was giving me a compliment! He just handed over the points I wanted because he perceived that I was confident in what I was going to say. He saw that I was "walking tall." I was never again irritated by the "*Wow, you're a lot shorter than I thought!*" comments. I just smile and think "*Yep, I am. And now that I know that you've seen me walking tall... I know you'll go more readily to where I'm leading you!*"

Confidence Killers!

There are lots of confidence killers lurking around us. Some are quite obvious: failing at some significant or public initiative, or people who we supported and trusted turning away from us. There are also the smaller blows that combined can grow into lethal monsters. These smaller blows include having insufficient knowledge about what we're doing and needing to move forward anyway, needing to switch positions or plans in a New-York minute, or sometimes just having a really bad hair day.

It does seem that more than anything, we don't want to look foolish. If there is one, single category of confidence-killing, doing something (anything!) that makes us seem dumb or silly is the worst. It's as though one moment will freeze in time and color everyone else's perception of us from that point forward. We often go through extraordinary amounts of effort to avoid looking foolish. I once read a horrifying story of a doctor who got a chicken bone caught in his throat while he was out dining with friends. Rather than look dumb at the table attempting to cough it up, he went to the men's room and choked to death because he had no one to help him. It would have been a lot better for him to look foolish!

Frame the hits to your self-confidence in the context of "what's the worst that can happen?" I believe the following Life Lesson illustrates about the worst that can happen. If you haven't had to live through this...then whatever else happens to you...you and your self-confidence can survive.

Life Lesson #13: Keep Your Pants On!

Before this story begins, I feel the need to explain the situation and supply my excuses up front.

Years ago when I was an independent consultant, I booked client engagements on the Tour from Hell. I committed myself to too many cities all over the country, too many client meetings and workshops, and too many hotels back to back. I was in my third different hotel (out of seven total) when I first said to myself, *"Jeanne, have you lost your mind? What did you do to yourself?"* But it was too late. The proverbial train had left the station—I was on my way.

After I had been on the road for two and a half weeks straight without returning home for R&R (or clean underwear) and had crossed all U.S. time zones three times, I could visualize a faint glimmer of the light on my own front porch. I was almost finished with this craziness. I was going home in only two more days! I had just started my last gig on the Tour from Hell. Just two more days in Atlanta and when Friday night came, I would be on my way back home to Orange County, California.

Then the phone rang. It was my favorite client asking me to please, please, please go there on Saturday morning to work with his project team. He said they were approaching a difficult phase of their project and had lost confidence in their ability to pull it off successfully. He needed me to help him stabilize and re-build his team. My exhausted body and good sense were screaming, *"NO!"* but my mouth said, *"Yes."* I got off the phone and worked on talking myself into believing that things would be okay. They were my favorite client...it was only one more event and one more day...I've always been able to find one more pittance of energy from somewhere...besides, Saturday work was premium pay!

I arrived in Oakland, California, from Atlanta, around midnight on Friday night. I was so exhausted that I could barely speak, but when I did, it came out super-crabby. The room I was given at the hotel was straight down the hall from the conference rooms where my meeting would take place. The front desk clerk gave me this information like it was an advantage. No, I did **not** want that room. I did **not** want to open my door and see hordes of people—some of whom I knew would be in my group—before I had to face them in the meeting. But there was no more room at the Inn. It was right off the conference area or sleep under a bridge. Okay, fine! I stomped away from the desk muttering loudly.

Even though I was tired, I immediately fell into my night-before-a-client-meeting preparation. I laid out my notes for the meeting so that I could run my eyes across them first thing in the morning. I laid out all the clothes I would wear and re-packed everything else. I fell into bed at 1:30 a.m., hoping I could "sleep fast."

It wasn't fast enough. When morning came, I thought I could not live through the day. I had to keep chanting my Little Engine Who Could mantra over and over: *"I think I can, I think I can. It's just one more day, Jeanne. You can do this!"* While I showered and dressed for the day, I focused intensely on convincing myself that I could not only show up, I could also do a good job.

I opened my door to find what I had suspected the night before. The hall was filled with people chattering, getting their pre-meeting coffee, getting in my way. I had to get to the end of the long hall and past all those people to put my suitcase into my rental car. (I was eagerly anticipating a fast getaway once I was finished with the meeting.) I chanted to myself again, *"You can do this. You can get past this crowd, and you can be convivial and polite. You don't need to stop and visit with them...just be nice."* I took a deep breath and began walking the gauntlet, pulling my suitcase and computer bag behind me. I was obviously not Moses, and the Red Sea of people did not instantly part. I smiled pleasantly and kept repeating *"Good morning. Excuse me. Good morning, excuse me,"* as I wove in and out of the tightly-packed crowd.

When I got to the exit where I had parked my car and opened the door, I felt a strange rush of cold air. I looked around and then down to discover that...**I had no pants on!** Yes, you have read this correctly. **No pants!** I was wearing panty hose with (thankfully!) hot pink panties underneath. My short red sweater jacket only came to my waist. Not only did the sweater not cover much—it didn't even match my panties! (Insult to injury!)

Could this be real? Have I really just walked past all these people without my pants? Yes, it was so terribly real.

I stood there with my back to the crowd (how terrible is **that** pose?!) for what seemed like an eternity trying to will myself to just die on the spot. But I didn't, and I suddenly knew where those pants where—hanging in the closet in the room at the other end of that people-packed hall. I had to go back. Amazingly, this time I did not have to say, *"Excuse me,"* even one time. Without a sound, the crowd simply parted for me instantly. With my head down, I walked through the hordes and back to my room as quickly as I could while still dragging along the luggage and computer bag. Yep...the pants were there ...hanging right where I had left them the night before.

I went into instant denial. *"This did not happen. It was just a bad dream. I think I'll just take my bags with me through the back way to the restaurant to meet my client for breakfast. Not that I **can't** walk through that crowd again...nothing happened to stop me. I just don't feel like it."* Denial, denial, denial—you are my friend! This approach worked until after breakfast, when it all came rushing back to me and I had to 'fess up. I just knew my client would hear about this from someone. It would be better if it was me.

I went through the whole scenario with him. When I came to, *"I didn't have my pants on,"* he breathed in quickly and his eyes became the size of dinner plates. We just looked at each other for a few seconds, until he literally fell off of his chair onto the floor laughing! Hmmm…I was so glad he was amused. I still wanted to die. But at least I wasn't kicked off the job. (That was me trying to find a positive spin on this.)

Minutes later, I had to face his team. I was sure that some (many/ all?) of them had been spectators (voyeurs?) to my earlier "per-formance." I said nothing about the incident until just before the first break. Then I could no longer ignore their too-wide eyes and repressed grins. I asked, *"Did anything unusual happen this morn-ing that you'd like to discuss?"* The group of twenty people sat perfectly still and silent, with even bigger eyes. Finally, one man said, *"You just lived my worst nightmare."* I responded with, *"I'm so glad that I could take that burden from you."*

At that point, the class erupted into exclamations of, *"That was unbelievable! How can you get through this? I couldn't believe my eyes! Good thing you were wearing panties!* (From a woman in the group!) *That was the most embarrassing thing that could ever happen to someone!* (Like I didn't know that?)" It was obvious that even those who hadn't actually witnessed the horror had heard about it. I couldn't think of an appropriate way to quell the chattering, so I just stood there and waited for the noise to stop. Finally, one of the men stood up. He said, *"I've been thinking about what happened a lot.* (Snickers from the group, which he and I ignored.) *No, not that! I mean, I figured that if you showed up for this meeting after what happened, then it would be some kind of sign. If you could live through that and face us, then we can live through what we have to do too."* The team instantly silenced while they processed that Life Lesson. I was so grateful for the man's intervention that I wanted to take him home and adopt him! Finally I asked the group, *"Is he right? If I lived through this, can you live through what you have to do?"* They all nodded their heads in agreement, and we had a productive and successful rest of the day.

My husband was less than thrilled when I told him the story that night when I finally landed at home. Before I left for the next several business trips, he felt it necessary to say, "*Now, please make sure that you don't forget to put everything on.*"

Those annoying reminders aside, I knew that I had learned and possibly taught an important Life Lesson. "*If it's not this bad...it ain't that bad.*" Somehow, we can dig deep and find the self-confidence we need to recover and go on. We just have to reach hard for it sometimes. We have to remember that, except for that one aberration, we're still okay.

Confidence Builders!

Confidence-building for leaders is a two-step process. Step One is building, sustaining, and re-building confidence in yourself. It involves taking care of yourself first so that you can care for others. It's just like real love. Love yourself first, and then you can love someone else. Step Two is building, shoring up, and supporting your followers' confidence.

Step One (A) in Building Confidence: It's All About You

The examination of personal confidence-building in this chapter of *Pink Leadership* comes with an assumption. You must already have a layer of personal confidence or you wouldn't have aspirations of becoming or enhancing your position as a superior leader. If you didn't already believe in yourself and your abilities, you likely wouldn't be reading *Pink Leadership*.

You can (and must!) protect, nurture, and build on the level of self-confidence that you already possess to ensure that you are always ready and well-positioned to do what you do…lead others well. Your "I'm okay" attitude will be tested often as a leader. There are many opportunities for you to feel like you are lower than an earthworm and you should just eat dirt. Don't do it! Remember: to lead others, you must feel good about yourself. To begin and maintain…it's all about you!

In a recent workshop I conducted on consulting skills, I offered that, *"We learn what is required to excel from both our successes and our failures."* A participant proposed that we learn more from our failures than from our successes and that we should focus more on the examination of the failures to know how to succeed. No…I just can't agree with that. Where does the confidence-building come in? If I'm busy looking at everything I did wrong with a jeweler's loupe, I will soon find myself wallowing in the ugliness of *"I'm not worthy."* That's no way for a leader to act! Yes, we do have to examine our mistakes for the purpose of knowing why and how we went off track. We want to listen to ourselves so that we can try hard not to make that particular mistake again. But too often we dwell on our mistakes or shortcomings and risk believing that we are the source of all things wrong.

> At one point in my varied career paths, I had aspirations of becoming a doctor. (Now you know the reason for my Biology/Chemistry majors when I returned to school. For a number of complicated reasons, I was unable to follow through on that dream.) One of the decisions I had to make while I was still pursuing the medical career, was the specialty I wanted to pursue. In a great example of a poor decision-making process, I first eliminated the fields that focused on body parts I didn't particularly like. Urology, Gastroenterology, and Podiatry came off my list first. I told my mentor that I also did not want to become a surgeon because they are just too arrogant for my taste. I didn't want to be like them. My mentor smirked and commented that I already had

a good foundation of being arrogant, so at least the step to "surgeon arrogance" would not be a quantum leap. (Hmmm...what nerve to say that to **me**!) My mentor then went on to address my notion that surgeons are arrogant. He said, "*Imagine a busy surgery morning. You have three operations scheduled one after another. For different reasons, the first two patients die. You probably didn't kill them, but you are the one standing there with the scalpel in your hand. You still have one to go. Just how confident do you have to be to have the courage to walk into that third operating room? You'd better have a huge reserve to draw from or you will not be able to make the decisions you need to make when you get in there. You call that arrogance. I call it a strong need to believe in yourself in order to save others.*"

What I heard was: "*If I'm going to suffer some major hits on my confidence, I'd better protect that self-esteem so that I can go on effectively.*" Also, I should stop complaining about surgeons being arrogant and be thankful when I have a super-confident doctor working on me or my family!

What does it take to sustain your self-confidence? A short list of actions includes the following:

- ▶ Look objectively at your mistakes and make a commitment or a plan to overcome or avoid them the next time the occasion arises. This will allow you to go beyond the small (or even larger) failures with renewed energy.

- ▶ Examine with delight the small victories. Don't gloat over them; but do see, feel, touch, and smell the sweetness of something you have done well. If you remember the good times, you will find in yourself the confidence to head in that direction again.

▶ Seek the counsel and company of those who care about you and in whom you place trust. Talk to them about your concerns and listen carefully to their replies. They are likely to see you more clearly than you see yourself.

▶ Do, wear, or see something that makes you feel good. For example, my office is filled with photographs of gorgeous flowers that my husband has taken and framed. (I do mean filled! I have 23 incredible photos on just one wall!) They make me smile every time I see them. I know that I'm okay when I'm surrounded by beautiful things.

Whatever works for you—whatever makes you feel vital and confident—that's what you should have. You need it, and you deserve it. It's all about you.

Step One (B) in Building Confidence: Practice Recovering

There is a long list of events and factors that assault our self-confidence. They can come flying in unexpectedly and smack us right between the eyes, or they can creep up quietly and insidiously, nibbling away at the core of our self-esteem. Either way—the result is not pretty. When we are strong, we can weather the small hits, unless there are just too many of them in too short a time. (Remember: "*That which does not kill you simply weakens you for the next blow.*") When we have been weakened, even less-significant, smaller attacks on our self-confidence can seem lethal. To continue to lead effectively, we have to learn to recover. Knowing how to recover effectively and quickly requires practice. It's not something that we're just born knowing how to do.

Regaining your personal confidence after a major blow or a cumulative assault of stinging jabs takes time, the support of others, and sometimes, a little luck in timing. With even a sideways glance from Lady Luck, something good will happen for you that will help to bring you back. However, you may not even notice the small good things unless you position yourself mentally and emotionally to seek them out. It's hard to see the glitter or hear the applause if you're head-down, scratching in the dirt with the chickens!

To get yourself well-positioned for the Recovery Run, listen to your own previous victory tapes in your mind and relive the successes and the feel-good times. Be around people who accept and admire you unconditionally. (If those people are in short supply, get a dog. You **can** buy unconditional, non-judgmental love!) Set your sights a little lower for a while. Go after something you know you can get. (Remember, if you don't get what you want, change what you want.) Celebrate more often the smaller victories. When you're beating yourself up because you don't know **everything**, a good thing to remember is that "in the land of the blind, one eye is king."

Can you recover and regain your emotional footing and self-confidence? Yes, you can. Just keep your pants on. If you're not showing your butt to a crowd of strangers, just how bad could it be?

The best confidence-recovery technique is to teach, support, and help someone else to grow. Move away from focusing on yourself and kill those dirt-scratching chickens you've been hanging out with. (I say that metaphorically. I have nothing against chickens.) The surest way to build confidence in yourself is to build it in others. By guiding, supporting, and watching someone else's development, you have validation of your own worth and contribution.

Step Two in Building Confidence: It's All About Them

As a "working" leader, you likely have several follower candidates around you who need your support. As a person, you've been focusing on taking care of yourself. The reason you are doing that, as a superior leader, is to be able to provide the quality leadership that your followers want and need.

How can you help others to help themselves?

► **Be patient.** Your followers' timetable is probably not the same as yours. They may not hear or see what they need to do to grow themselves in the time frame that you think is appropriate. But this part is all about them. They need to set the pace for their own advancement. (Don't let them take forever, however. Forever delay is actually resistance, not required growth time. Consciously think about how long you believe it should take others to get over whatever it is they're wrestling with. Then double that time. If they aren't ready by then—they need a smack in the head.)

► **Provide good role modeling.** This is not the time to demonstrate or express your own insecurities unless you are using the examples for *"...and this is how you can overcome this challenge"* purposes.

► **Determine what they need to feel confident.** Do they need more personal skills training? If so, work to provide that for them, either in formal workshops or, if that's not possible, by suggesting some self-study avenues. (There are lots of quality self-study books on the market for personal skills development. Find them, hand them out, or strongly suggest that your followers buy them. While you're at it, you may as well read them yourself.)

Do they need more focused coaching? If so, discuss the options with your person. Maybe they'll want you to practice them before a presentation or critique their written memos to others. (It's important that you reach agreement on the level and timing of coaching. If you don't, you can be perceived as putting your nose where it doesn't belong.)

Do they need a different mentor? There have been occasions when, in order to help someone else, I've had to step away from that person and recruit a different mentor. I could tell that we were not the best fit for each other. In those cases, we've talked it over together, and I've enlisted someone else to work with the person. Providing good leadership sometimes means knowing when to let go!

▶ **Recognize your people's achievements and help them to see, hear, and feel the applause.** Help to build their confidence by letting them savor the glory of accomplishment and your approval. What would your reaction be if you received this quick e-mail from your leader/mentor when you had done something well? *"Have I told you lately that I think you are TOO FINE? If I haven't, I should have!"* You would likely feel very good about yourself. Your people will too when you send an acknowledgment like this.

Sometimes the recognition is small—a smile and a wink, a quick note, a pat on the back—and sometimes, it can be life-changing, if that's what the occasion or the accomplishment warrants.

Life Lesson #14: The Mouse That Roared

This story takes place in the Netherlands at the business school that I designed and taught in for a large European software company. Every ten-week semester, we would have 30 to 50 new students from software and consulting firms around the world. The training was all conducted in English although each class had up to 17 different "first languages" sitting in the same room. (English was the third or fourth language for some of the attendees, which made the classes challenging for them and also for the trainers!)

During one semester, my husband and I were teaching many of the classes together, and we had lucked out in the language department. Everyone in the class spoke passable English, except for one young man from Japan. For nine of the ten weeks, the young man sat silently at the back of the room, watching and presumably listening. The only sound from him was the whirring of the pages of his Japanese-English dictionary. (I'd never seen anyone who could leaf through pages as fast as he could!) Despite repeated attempts, we could not connect with the young man. We had no idea if he grasped anything that was going on in the classes. Bill and I, and the rest of the class, just let him be there—every day, in the back of the room, quietly flipping through his dictionary.

The Finals Week was an intense culmination and demonstration of everything the students had studied in the previous nine weeks. The class was divided into teams, each of which was given a complex client case study. The assignment was to identify the business problems and determine the business process and software solutions. The teams then had to prepare a team demonstration and present their recommendations to a panel of judges that included university professors, high-ranking corporate executives, other "heavy hitters" from field operations, and my husband and me. Bill and I (along with other trainer/consultants from my company) observed the teams' preparations and graded their demonstrated skills and abilities as they were working together. The teams would be graded and ranked against each other at the end of the week, and a winning team would be selected. The members of the winning team were always given raises, promotions, and plum assignments. There was a lot on the line for the class teams. The Finals Week was a major factor in determining the direction of their career paths, and they knew it!

Bill was watching his team, which included the quiet young man from Japan, as they began to build their PowerPoint presentation on the second day of Finals Week. (They were doing this too soon, since they didn't have their solution defined yet, but Bill had to let them figure out this mistake for themselves.) The rest of the team was ignoring the presence of their Japanese colleague just as we all had for the previous nine weeks. Who knew if he was even following what they were doing? He was just the mouse in the corner. While the others wordsmith-ed and argued about colors and the order of the slides, he was tap, tap, tapping on his computer. Suddenly, the young man got up and went to the front of the room, carrying his computer. He gestured for permission to project the image he wanted to show the team. In amazement at his sudden participation, Bill gestured for him to proceed.

The young man had created **one** slide—the best one any of us had ever seen. It graphically explained the entire software and business solution with just one image! The depth of the young man's own understanding was evident, along with his incredible ability to simplify a complex concept. Everyone in the room was silenced in awe of what they were seeing—they all stared with saucer eyes. The Japanese student wasn't sure if he should remain in the spotlight because no one spoke, and he tried to retreat to his corner. But Bill wouldn't let him.

Bill told the young man to stay where he was and then went in search of one of the company executives so that he could see the amazing graphic. Bill located the CEO who accompanied him back to the classroom, which created a wave of "celebrity-appearance" excitement. The CEO immediately saw the value of the Japanese man's graphic, walked over to him, and bowed deeply in appreciation.

For the next three days, Bill was glued to the Japanese "mouse's" side—almost 24/7! They were like Mutt and Jeff—6'2" Bill and his side-kick, the 5'3" student from Japan. Bill encouraged, connected with, and coached the young man aggressively. Time was running out! Bill had to focus his attention quickly to build this young man's recognition of and confidence in his own abilities.

At the formal graduation, the Japanese man's team did not win first place. During the proceedings, however, the CEO asked Bill and the former "mouse" to come to the front of the room. He then showed the PowerPoint to the entire audience, which numbered over 200 with the executives from all the companies that had sent students. The CEO announced that the graphic was to be the symbol and standard for his company going forward. In addition, the concept of "making the difficult easy" that was demonstrated in the design would henceforth be the guiding message for the company. The CEO also pointed out that Bill was the one who *listened and watched and found our super star for us.*" Our Japanese student was to receive very generous rewards in title, compensation, and assignment in the company—along with intensive English language training. Bill did not need an additional reward. His delight for his student was obvious!

Immediately after the ceremony concluded, Bill's student hurried to his side. He bowed very deeply and slowly, and said, "*I will never forget. You changed my life.*" Bill returned the bow, and both men stood there for some time while they worked hard to hold back their tears.

There are so many Life Lessons in this story:

- *Listen and watch for the value in others.*

- *Don't assume that because someone is different in race, language, color, size, or age, that she or he is not worthy of your time and attention.*

- *Be ready to teach, coach, mentor, and build confidence in worthy followers.*

- *Give of yourself without looking for a personal reward. Just do it for the benefit of someone else.*

- *Never forget that your role as a leader is both to inspire others to be confident of your direction and also to help build your followers' personal confidence.*

While you are building, sustaining, and re-building your confidence as a leader, what's the next step? The next step is to use it...be brave...just do it!

CHAPTER 12

Just Do It!

*Leaders take the calculated risks that others may not be ready to try and then provide the support so that followers may also be as **brave** as their leaders are.*

B RAVERY IS THE last leadership characteristic that we're going to explore. Bravery is the scary characteristic because it's the element that is an "action item." If you do not demonstrate bravery, then your enthusiasm and passion, trustworthiness and honesty, authenticity and respectfulness, comfort and calm, and confidence may be for naught.

There are lots of inspirational quotes to help motivate you to get to the end-game—the achievement of the desired outcomes of your leadership. These include the following:

- ▶ *"If you can see it, you can achieve it."*
- ▶ *"More often than not, those who win believe they can."*
- ▶ *"The first and most important step to success is the feeling that we can succeed."*
- ▶ *"You just need to have the vision and the dream."*

There are an incredible number of these motivational sayings that seem to imply that "if we want it bad enough, it will just happen for us."

Not! While I am not discounting the need to believe in ourselves and to be able to picture success, confidence and visualization alone are not the magic bullets that will result in your leadership success. You must also **do** something. Whenever you really do something, you are using your bravery because you are putting yourself, your ideas, your time, and your energy at risk. You are not just saying, *"This is good. I want it, and I can achieve it."* You are also saying, with your actions, *"And I will make this happen by my effort, my actions, and my leadership."*

What is the hardest part of "doing something?" It's getting started! This means overcoming the inertia (and often the fatigue!) that we all suffer. We may believe strongly in our objectives, and we may be cognitively committed to the attainment of our goals. But sometimes, when we have a large initiative or too many of them (of any size) on our plates concurrently, we may not be able to make the emotional commitment. We just don't feel like it! We say (quietly and only to ourselves), *"Yeah, this is great all right. But it's going to kill me to do it. I'll start this…later."* But sometimes, "later" never comes. We dream, we visualize, we plan, we want to be brave and do whatever it is…but we just can't seem to start. We just can't seem to take that first step.

What's Holding You Back?

If you just can't seem to get started, look around to find the barricades. What is holding you back? Is it fatigue? If that's the problem, figure out how to get some rest or reprieve. Delegate or re-prioritize, lie on the couch for an entire afternoon, eat better and exercise a little—do whatever it takes to renew your energy. Rebuilding your own energy may be the first and most significant step on your task list. Prepare yourself to be brave enough to jump into the rest of the plans.

Another barricade to our starting can be the magnitude of the task at hand—either real or the way we perceive it. Some endeavors seem worthwhile and we want to lead toward their success, but they appear to be just too big! We may see an obscenely large number of steps that have to be taken, or the personal risk may seem inordinately great, or the calendar time may stretch out too long for our attention and patience levels.

> For as long as I can remember, people have been telling me, "*You need to write a book. You should be capturing all these stories for other people.*" Although I had written a large number of articles, white papers, essays, short stories, marketing brochures, and educational workbooks, I had never attempted to write a book. The "distance" of a book seemed too great for me. I'm often too focused on the end—I like things to be done! On a rational level, I finally committed to go from writing smaller pieces to writing books. But I just couldn't start. I talked often at home about what I wanted and was going to do, but I wouldn't put my hands on the keyboard. Finally, my husband (who knows me so well!) said, "*Maybe you should drink your own Kool-Aid—do what you tell others to do. Break that book-writing down to smaller tasks. You don't have to sit down and do the whole thing at once. Check off your task list one item at a time.*" What a concept—listen to my own advice! After three months of procrastination, I listened to Bill and took my own counsel. I defined the steps, looked at the reality of the task ahead of me, and began to work through the list. Once I started, I found I even enjoyed the process—something that I had once felt was just too great a stretch in time and effort for me.

Find a Reason to Get Started

Encouraging you to get started is not a contradiction to the imperative to stop working too long and too hard and to pace appropriately. Sometimes the challenge is finding the motivation and the self-discipline to focus on the right tasks. It is so much easier and more pleasant, and safer, to while away the time on something we want to do, something that may be easy or more pleasant for us, rather than focus on things we *have* to do.

Sometimes you need to find motivation to focus your attention and effort on an initiative even when you might want to and believe you should. You just can't get it high enough on the priority list. You need some stimulus—a jump start.

In some instances, breaking down the enormity of your task will work for you. In other situations, you'll need to "trick" yourself to get started.

Life Lesson #15: Powder Puff Mechanics

I spent a large part of my young adult life in northern Minnesota, in Hibbing and Pengilly (on the Iron Range) and in Duluth—where it's always "colder by the lake." I know that northern Minnesota has many appealing attributes, but they don't readily come to my mind. What I remember most are the mosquitoes, the snow, and the incredible, "if-you-stop-moving-you-will-die" cold in the winter. With the killer cold came irritating, time-consuming requirements just to live and move around—like putting on boots all the time, and shoveling snow, and trying to get your car started. I hated the car-starting part the most. (This was before the advent of engine heaters and ubiquitous electrical cords hanging out of the front grills of cars like slightly obscene appendages.)

The standard process when my car wouldn't start was to ask some man to make it start. I found that you could ask just about any man, as they all seemed to know the secret. It was definitely a guy thing. My male rescuer would open the hood, reach in and touch something, and then tell me, "*Okay, now try it.*" Most of the time, this approach worked, and it was **so** irritating to me! I hated the dependency, the feeling of impotence, and I especially hated not knowing what the rescuer was touching. What was that magic thing that made the car start for him? I knew I had to find out.

Not long after my husband Bill and I were married, I came home and announced excitedly, *"I'm going to find out how to make the car start by myself! I enrolled at the Voc-Tech in a class called Powder Puff Mechanics."* (I really did **not** like the name of the class. I asked the school if they would consider changing it, but that didn't appear to be an option. Oh well, if it taught me the car-starting secret, I could work to get past the name.) Bill's reaction did not match my excitement; in fact, he was not even very pleasant.

"Why would you enroll in a class like that?" he asked with undisguised irritation. I hastened to remind him of how much I hated not being able to start my own car. I threw in arguments of my personal safety. *"But,"* he protested, *"I can teach you everything you need to know in a few Saturday mornings in our own garage."* Arrgghh…I heard what the problem was, and it was another guy thing. I had, from his perspective, announced that I was going to be unfaithful. I was going to another man to find out about my car, guy stuff—the mysteries that he knew everything about.

But still I pitched my case. *"But I won't do it. I won't go into the garage on Saturday and get my hands dirty if I don't have a class I need to go to and a test to pass."* Bill's response was both flattering and untrue. With a loving smile, he said, *"Of course you will. You're highly motivated to learn this, and I'm certain that you'll follow through with it."* There was no appropriate comeback for that compliment—I had lost the argument, and quickly. I cancelled Powder Puff Mechanics, did **not** get my $49 registration back, and selected my outfit to wear in our own garage for my first lesson. But when that Saturday came, and the next Saturday and the next, I was too busy with some other project *du jour* to go out to the garage. I never did learn what those men were touching under the hood.

It was several years before I realized that I had learned a valuable Life Lesson from this incident. I didn't immediately analyze why I never went out to our garage for my lessons or how that applied to other initiatives I wanted to take on but didn't. Over time, I came to understand that even when I wanted or needed to do something, sometimes it was too tedious, ugly, or risky to just jump in there and do it. The Life Lesson is: *You may have to include steps in the process that will force you to be brave and just do it.*

Lead and Manage Yourself

To ensure that we've adequately covered the topic of "getting started," we have to include one more reason: self-discipline. Although this reason is not related to how brave you are, it is definitely a factor in our inertia. What a revelation that self-discipline is not fun—like you didn't already know that! It may be fulfilling when you've done it well and when you have something to show for your effort. However, summoning up the discipline to make ourselves start something that is less-than-appealing is sometimes like poking yourself in the eye. Just not something that you want to do!

There may be times when you have to "trick" yourself to get from *"I just don't feel like doing this"* to *"Okay, it's not going to kill me...I'll just do it."*

I really hate cooked spinach—it's too soggy and flaccid and the color is too green. I never cook it or order it, but occasionally it appears on my plate at a dinner at some friend's or family member's house. (This seemed to happen a lot more when I lived in northern Minnesota.) It's been given to me, so I have to eat it or risk appearing ungrateful. When this unfortunate situation arises, I **always** eat the spinach first. I get it out of the way, and I feel wonderful about myself just because I did it. I can then enjoy the rest of the meal much more because I'm not dreading a confrontation with the green stuff—and it's not getting colder (and uglier) while it sits there, taunting me. Almost all new leadership requirements have spinach. There is some action that you just don't want to take—such as calling your list of people, setting up the spreadsheet to track progress, or writing up the proposal that you didn't think was even necessary in the first place. Whatever you dread—that is your spinach. Eat it first and savor the small victory. Getting the spinach off your plate will help you eagerly attack the next, and hopefully more pleasant, steps in your initiative. Sometimes you just need to eat the spinach first.

Be Willing to Take the Risk(s)

Leaders are, by the nature of what they do, risk-takers. They see and work toward the fulfillment of a vision and they effect change. They often take an unpopular stance. They have to be the first to step out on the limb and the first to jump in the water.

Getting started, and being willing to continue the quest, often means putting yourself at risk. If your leadership actions do not involve any personal risk, then your sights are likely not yet high enough. It is often true that risk increases as a function of the magnitude of the rewards: the greater the rewards, the higher the risk. We hear often, *"Aim for the moon, because even if you miss, you will land among the stars."* That's well and good, but you might get pretty beat up in the meantime! Are you willing to take that chance? Are you brave enough? If you are a leader, you must be that brave.

One of my favorite quotes provides some additional motivation to the challenge of putting myself at risk. *"You can't cross the sea merely by standing and staring at the water.*"[12] It's telling that of all the quotes that speak to getting started and taking on the risks of action, this is my favorite. A confession—I'm afraid of water. Well, not exactly the water—I'm afraid of what might be *in* the water. I don't go on boats and I don't swim where there isn't a concrete bottom. That's why this quote speaks so loudly to me. It reminds me that sometimes I have to overcome my greatest fears to achieve a worthy goal. I must jump into the water and be brave enough to fight off whatever ugly thing is in there, or I'll just end up on the beach—likely alone and certainly unfulfilled.

The personal risk is exactly that—very personal. What is risky for you may be "easy-schmeasy" for someone else. What you are afraid of, what you believe you are "putting on the line," is entirely your call. In my role as a strategist, I've often been the person who has to deliver the bad news to others. I've had to tell C-level executives that their people don't trust them. I've had to reset other colleagues' or clients' expectations about what could or should be done. These actions often mean that the receivers of the bad news will not like me. I risk not being accepted and/or liked every time I am the messenger of "gloom." This is a small risk for me. I have enough friends. This risk will not stop me from moving forward on what I know has to be done. But it might stop you.

If you believe that putting yourself in a position of not being accepted or liked is a potentially, and seriously, self-damaging risk, then it is. The chance of not being too popular because of the initiative that you're undertaking may be what you are putting on the line. You will want to weigh whatever you perceive as your personal risk against the benefits, determine how to mitigate the risk, and then move forward. You will likely discover that your anticipation of the personally negative outcome is worse than the reality, and you will be able to

---

[12] This quote is attributed to Rabindranath Tagore, an Indian poet, playwright, and essayist, who won the Nobel Prize for Literature in 1913.

overcome your own fear of your identified risk much easier the next time it comes around.

Objectively weighing the risks against the benefits often requires the counsel of someone you trust. Enhancing your own bravery often means reaching out to others for their help. This is a situation when the need to select the right mentor becomes very clear. (See Chapter 2 about avoiding the Pyrite Devils. Select a brave leader-mentor who will help you to be brave also.)

Occasionally, mitigating the risk means putting more preparation or effort into your actions. I may not be really concerned about being liked, but I am afraid of the risk of letting others down. If (read more truthfully: when) I have done that, it's personally damaging to me and requires lots of work to rebuild my own courage to wade into something where that risk exists again. It's not that I just don't like to let others down. To me, this is a great personal risk in large part because I fear the personal pain that I will feel at letting others down, which is a *very* big deal to me. (See Chapter 9 and the Veni, Vidi, Vici story. That tells you where my fear comes from!) When I'm faced with an initiative that I perceive involves too many people who are dependent on me for too much, I just don't want to do it! However, if the benefit is great enough, I know that I must. I must prepare what has to be done very well, allow sufficient time to accomplish the task, set (and often re-set) expectations with followers, and talk myself out of believing that every small "failure" is a death blow.

Sometimes the risk is great because we are venturing into the unknown. Who knows what evils are lurking out there, just waiting to get us? There are (thankfully!) few occasions when we need to demonstrate bravery in leadership by putting our lives at risk. Unless you're a leader in a war zone, or heading up a rescue mission in the Rocky Mountains, your tasks are usually not life-endangering extreme. But the unknown can be perceived as close-to-death. We don't know if it will kill us...because we don't know what it is!

A few years after starting my consulting firm, Key Performance International, I hired my sister, Pattie Erpenbach, to work as a professional skills consultant and trainer. I hired her away from the May Company where she was working as a computer programmer. Pattie was really venturing into unknown territory when she was brave enough to go from COBOL programming to teaching presentation skills to executives! Pattie didn't have the education or the experience in doing what I wanted her to do, but she had all the personal characteristics that I knew were essential for the position. She had a willingness and ability to connect with others, empathy, integrity, patience, intelligence, and a strong work ethic, and she demonstrated other signs of being a high-quality leader. Unfortunately, at the time, she was also cowardly about lots of little things. (Until her late twenties, she refused to drive over bridges!)

I didn't realize that, at 40+ years old, Pattie had never flown over water, checked into a hotel by herself, or rented a car—and, more importantly, was afraid to do any of that. She sure had to get through those fears in a hurry! When she had been working for me for the "extended period" of two weeks, I told her she needed to fly to Europe. She didn't share with me the monster anxieties that she suffered on that first trip for a long time. I heard about the trauma after she had conquered her fears, which was about six months later after she had made several more trips back and forth to Europe, checked into many hotels, rented cars, crossed lots of bridges, and driven around several countries where she couldn't understand the road signs.

Whenever I was sending a new employee, who had not traveled internationally before, to anywhere outside the United States, I tried to make sure they had everything they needed to survive—and even enjoy—the experience. I made sure that they had maps and translation dictionaries and I supplied them with lots of tips about "things to watch out for." I alerted them about the co-ed bathrooms in France, the absence of doughnuts just about everywhere, giving the hotel keys back to the desk clerk every day and having to retrieve them when they returned, only ordering Bisleri bottled water in India, and police with rifles and bullet-proof vests at the airports. We practiced together the "polite" words in every language and spent time discussing how **not** to be perceived as an ugly American. Because of my personal prejudice against "weird" food, I also warned them not to eat anything that had the word "Carpaccio" in the name. Carpaccio means **raw**—beef, lamb, trout, who-knows-what-else—all of it **raw!** (Many of you reading this may like that stuff. And if you do, then you just go for it! No raw meat is passing my lips, and I don't think anyone else should be eating it either. Yes, I know, that's a control issue.)

A few years after Pattie began her world travels, there were five of us working together in the Netherlands. We had all been invited to the home of one of our clients for his birthday party. We were very pleased to attend and proud that we had been asked to celebrate with the client's friends and family. (Birthdays are very important to the Dutch people, and being invited to a birthday celebration is no small honor in the Netherlands.)

At the party, our host was passing around appetizers and offered Pattie a plate with something unidentifiable. She reached out and touched whatever-it-was while she said pleasantly, *"Thank you very much. And, what is this?"* The response horrified her. *"It's Carpaccio of horse."* It's raw horse meat? She did **not** want to eat that!

With her fingers still touching the offered "treat" and her eyes like a deer in the headlights, Pattie quickly looked at me for advice. I nodded yes, almost imperceptibly. My subtle head bob meant, *"Yes, that really is horse!"* She interpreted it as, *"Yes, you must eat it."* While the rest of us watched in amazement, she said *"Austeblieft,"*[13] and ate it!

---

[13] *Austeblieft* has to be the most commonly used word in the Dutch language. It means, "Thank you, you're welcome, here it is, there ya' go, okay" and a host of other phrases. I've heard entire conversational exchanges between Netherlanders where the only word spoken was "austeblieft," and they both knew what the other person meant. It's certainly very efficient—which is also very Dutch— when you get used to it!

Our host moved on to his other guests, and the five of us sat in stunned silence, watching Pattie chew and chew and chew. When our host was out of earshot, I broke the silence by saying, *"You have just eaten Flicka."* One of our colleagues offered, *"It's like you walked up to Secretariat and took a bite out of his leg."* Pattie just stared straight forward...and chewed, while the rest of us erupted into inappropriate and barely concealed laughter!

I also said, as soon as I regained my composure, *"And you showed us how to be brave, and how to act properly when we're guests in a different culture."* Pattie didn't acknowledge or even recognize that praise right then. I think she was still chewing.

I was grateful for and will long remember the superior example of being brave, taking risks, and moving outside your own comfort zone in deference to another's needs that I had witnessed. I was also grateful at the time that Pattie managed to keep the Carpaccio down! (I was a little concerned about a potential ugly American display if the already-consumed horse meat ended up on the floor. But not to worry...Pattie was definitely "green around her gills," but Flicka stayed down!)

My instincts about Pattie's abilities and potential proved to be true. She is now one of the best skills trainers I've ever seen and a respected Personnel Practice Manager with CIBER. She will drive over bridges, ride the New York subway, and eat unfamiliar things—except Carpaccio of anything!

To Fight or Not to Fight...That Is the Question

There is little gender-specificity in this question. There are large numbers of people from both sexes who are conflicted about conflict—engage and fight or avoid/run/ignore and not fight. The fear of conflict is a very personal and compelling fear, and subsequently it's perceived as a very personal risk.

There are two distinct conflict camps: the fighters and the avoiders. My experience in working with and coaching others in professional skills tells me that there are more avoiders than there are fighters. The fighters are certainly more visible (and louder), which may lead us to believe that many people choose to engage in conflict. We're just being distracted by their noise. The avoiders at the far end of their side of the continuum will often go to extraordinary means, up to and including causing real damage to their careers (and to their mental and emotional well-being), to dodge conflict situations. In the other camp, the fighters will engage not only in appropriate conflicts that arise, they may also initiate disagreements just to have something to fight about. Certainly, neither extreme side of the fighter-avoider spectrum is a good place to be!

> I used to believe that my role in life was to "kill dragons." There were dragons everywhere attacking me and others who I cared about—and it was my job to rid the world of them. When Bill and I were about to be married, I asked him if he would help me fight off the dragons once we were married. His reply was, "*Of course, I will help you. I just wish you wouldn't stir them up so much first.*"

The ability of a leader to face and successfully resolve conflict is one of the most difficult skills to achieve and also the most valuable asset in a leader's tool bag. The fear of conflict and the skill sets required for positive conflict resolution are both so complex that deep-dive, comprehensive looks at these will be the subject of another book. But at a high level, if you feel the potential for conflict to arise in your leadership efforts is a significant risk to you, you will want to approach this barrier in the same way as any other challenge.

First, figure out what exactly you are afraid of. Is it the actual conflict itself or is it the process or the outcome that you fear? Perhaps disagreements can mean that others do or will not like you and you have a high need to be liked. You may not be as confident as you need to be and fear that a conflict will reveal that you are not "as advertised"—you aren't as "good" or as prepared as you need to be. Conflict may mean to you that someone "loses," and you are afraid that the loser will be you. (You may have been the "loser" in many conflicts growing up and learned to protect yourself by avoiding those incidents in your adulthood.) You may be extremely "soft-hearted" and feel the pain of others excessively. You may view conflict as a painful ordeal and are afraid of inflicting pain on others. You may be afraid that verbal conflict could escalate into physical conflict and you have a long-standing fear of that. It's not really the conflict itself that puts us at risk. Our sense of risk comes from how we feel about what is happening or what can happen as a result of the conflict.

Second step: once you have determined the real reason for your conflict avoidance, go after it! Stand up and look that particular devil in the eye! Think, prepare well, plan—do whatever it takes to overcome your fear. Over time, and with perfect practice, the perception of the risk will reduce. This is true! With practice, you will see that there are significant benefits to conflict situations, and you can become willing and able to step into appropriate and required frays in the interest of leading and succeeding. You need to try it to see if you will like it.

Spread the Love Around!

Concurrent with working on your own bravery, you will want to use your leadership skills to help your followers to be brave. You may note that I did not use the phrase "motivate others to be brave." I do not believe that we can motivate anyone to be brave, or to be or do much of anything else. Over the years, I have been billed on some speaking engagements as a "Motivational Speaker." I always cringe when I see that title next to my name because I feel more than a little fraudulent. Can I really motivate anyone with my presentation? I can possibly motivate others for 5 minutes after my talk or 50 yards beyond the door of the conference center, but beyond that...I'm not so sure. I don't know what really motivates others. Peter F. Drucker said, *"We know nothing about motivation. All we can do is write books about it."*

You (and I) may not be able to motivate others, but we can create the environment for them to self-motivate. We can encourage, demonstrate, coach, lead, and possibly inspire, but our followers' motivation has to come from within them, just as our own motivation is internal. Our followers have the right to make their own decisions and choose their own paths, just as we do. Dr. Seuss said it clearly. *"You have brains in your head. You have feet in your shoes. You can steer yourself in any direction you choose. You're on your own. And you know what you know. You are the guy who'll decide where to go."*

Along the path to bravery and getting things done, it is certainly discouraging when others are not as brave or hard-working or committed as you are. You may blame yourself or them, or you may point your finger at someone or something to get over your own disappointment. But, you are a leader. You recognize that you need to create the environment for your followers to be motivated enough to be as brave as you are. As a leader, you treat people authentically and with respect, which means accepting that others too have the right to make their own decisions, to change their minds, and to act on their own levels of risk comfort. In the interim, you will want and need to continue to work on your own bravery and also "share the love" with your followers.

Creating the environment that your followers need to build and sustain their own motivation means first working to identify the mental and/or emotional roadblocks (either real or perceived) that they may encounter. The second step is to work for and with your followers to remove these barriers. It's the same process that you use to identify and then remove your own barricades. The difference is that when you are supporting the bravery in others, you are outwardly focused. It's no longer about you—it's all about them. What do they need to feel brave? What can you do to help them become self-disciplined...to get started...to stay with the task? How can you make things easier for someone else? These are questions that you will need to answer for **your** followers. Almost all the answers are going to be unique to each team, group, or individual because your followers are all different people with varying needs and fears.

A basic tenet of building bravery (and motivation) is to make things as easy as you can for others. If something is not too hard... someone just might do it! Keeping people brave and motivated is easier than getting them started. (Just like with you!) Making things easier is usually a collection of small things. In Chapter 9, we explored doing the little things because the big things will follow. The same principle applies to making it easy for people to be brave and to do what you want and need to them do.

I offer a small suggestion for a very little thing that makes it easier for people to follow your lead. I'm seriously dependent on and addicted to e-mail and instant messaging. Almost all my mouth-to-ear communication is preceded by some written request to have the other person call me. Every time I ask for a call, I include my whole phone number with the area code. If I ask the same person three times in a day by instant messaging, I include the number three times. I don't want that person to have to look up my number; I want it to be as easy as I can make it for him or her to pick up the phone. So how does that help make them brave? The readily-supplied phone number may not. However, the combination and consistent regard for making things easier for others will accumulate and result in braver, more motivated, and more ready-to-jump-in-with-you followers. They won't be quick to believe it will be hard to follow your lead because you've demonstrated by the little things that are you willing to make things easy for them.

One element of support you can supply that is generally valuable to all of your followers is to role model bravery. The leader is the heartbeat of an organization, team, or family unit. The way your heart beats—strong, empathically, enthusiastically, honestly, and bravely is a significant factor to the way the hearts of your followers will beat. Inspiring others to be brave means being brave yourself and then doing what your followers need to make it easy, desirable, and rewarding to follow your lead.

CHAPTER 13
Who Is the Fairest of Them All?

I's HARD TO visualize the whole of a luxury car when we are looking at the headlights, wheels, seats, and engine in separate pictures. So far, that's what we have been doing—looking at what a leader is and does in separate pictures. Like a Porsche, the beauty and impact of the "whole" of a superior leader is always greater than the sum of the parts.

Good leaders possess these "parts":

▶ Enthusiasm and passion
▶ Trustworthiness and honesty
▶ Authenticity and respectfulness in their approach to others
▶ Comfort and calm with change or ambiguity
▶ Confidence
▶ Bravery

What do we see when we put all the pieces of a leader together and we are able to see the sum of her parts?

"...And a Child Shall Lead Us"

Christmas is a very big deal to me. I love everything about it—shopping, decorating, baking, attending Midnight Mass, hosting parties, and getting Christmas cards. (Well, maybe there's one thing I don't love. I almost never *send* Christmas cards—but I do receive them gratefully.)

One year, I planned a Christmas that was to be the "Big Christmas"—the holiday that would make all the others seem like "just a Tuesday afternoon." There were several reasons why this would be the Big Christmas: the Las Vegas contingent of our family had just swelled to 9 people, I planned a company party for all my employees at our home, and I invited all 14 of my entire scattered-around-the-country family to join us in Vegas to celebrate. And they all accepted the invitation! We were to host 23 to 37 people across a 12-day span. Three separate Christmas celebrations were on the agenda—one just for the Vegas family, one for the company guests, and one huge all-family Christmas package-opening event on Christmas Eve. I was a whirlwind for most of that year with all the planning, shopping, baking, decorating, and wrapping of gifts. I refused to even think about how tired and broke I was going to be after this event. ("Denial" was my attitude of choice.) I planned to and did enjoy every minute of the preparation!

One of my favorite Christmas activities is buying and wrapping gifts, and because it's high on my list of love-to-do's, my approach is just a little excessive. (I was once accused of using the telephone book as my Christmas gift list.) I was so excited about the Big Christmas and so ready for it to happen that I was completing the action items on my To-Do list well in advance of the due dates. This included baking 70 dozen cookies, decorating with so many lights that our yard rivaled the Vegas Strip, and, of course, wrapping all the gifts.

By Thanksgiving, I had bought and wrapped every gift. This was no small feat because there were over 150 presents! I carefully arranged them in my library in their respective piles according to date and package-opening event and guests. (My OCD was in full bloom. Yes, I also had a master inventory list by date, by guest, and by gift. I was seriously obsessed and happy to be that way!) The gifts couldn't go under the tree because there was no Christmas tree yet. Since the tree goes up the day after Thanksgiving, I arranged and re-arranged all the gifts several times to get them categorized, organized, and looking wonderful in their temporary location. The library was a cornucopia of conspicuous consumption in bright colors with made-by-hand bows.

My mother and step-father lived with my husband and me at the time and watched my frenzy with poorly-disguised concern for potential damage to my mental and physical well-being. I may have been enjoying the effort, but they feared that it would kill me (or them by proximity). Along the way, however, my every-night-for weeks wrapping efforts inspired my mother to begin her wrapping also. She wrapped the five gifts she had already purchased and piled them very nicely in the den. (I did not get my OCD-ness from my mother.)

Thanksgiving Day arrived. (I only cared about Thanksgiving that year because it was the day before the Christmas tree went up.) My daughter Julie and grand-daughter Carissa arrived at our house for Turkey Day and saw the advanced Christmas preparations for the first time. Carissa had hugged and kissed Grandma and Grandpa "P" (her great-grandparents) and cuddled with them for a few minutes in the den before she made her way to the library which was "all Christmas." Can you just imagine the look on five-year-old Carissa's face when she saw those 150+ gifts? Our always-chatty Carissa was momentarily (but only briefly) stunned into silence. She had found the mother lode! She went from package to package, carefully "petting" the boxes, exclaiming over the bows, and making little squealing sounds of delight.

After her intense review, Carissa turned to her mother, and said, *"Mommy, you should go and see what Grandma P has ready for Christmas too."* Carissa took Julie's hand to lead her to the den. As they left the library, I heard Carissa say, *"Now, Mommy, when you see Grandma P's presents, be real excited and remember—she did the best that she could."*

Now I was stunned into silence, and for quite a long time. While I had been consumed with the physical expressions of the Big Christmas, Carissa focused her attention on something much greater. I had never before witnessed such an incredible expression of love, kindness, and **leadership**—and it had come from a five-year-old! Carissa was demonstrating and encouraging enthusiasm and passion: *"...be real excited."* She was being honest, authentic, and respectful in her evaluation: *"...she did the best that she could."* She was comfortable, calm, confident, and brave enough to coach her mother on how she should react to the 5 versus 150 gifts.

In the years that have passed since that significant Life Lesson, I have never seen a more concise, but still all-inclusive, example of true leadership. I knew when I heard it, and I remember when I often recall that wonderful moment, that "...a child shall lead us."

Pink Leadership has provided stories about real people in real-life situations that may be similar to those that you have experienced. The people I've written about are not celebrities or instantly-recognizable super stars. They are just like you and me. Along the way they have graced my life with the powerful examples to listen to, to watch, and to learn from. Because a leader is also a mentor, coach, and teacher, I've shared the Life Lessons with you so that you may listen and learn and then mentor, coach, and teach others well.

Of all the exceptional people whom I've met and who have provided me with priceless Life Lessons, there are two in particular that you may choose to remember and emulate.

In Chapter 1, you met Lemma Gailani, who not only possesses the foundational characteristics of a good leader, but who is also willing to work hard to enhance and then apply those traits to quality leadership. I'm confident that she will continue to embrace the effort and the sacrifices that she must in order to continue traveling down her chosen path to success. Lemma is a learner and a "try-er," and a fighter. She will put herself at risk to achieve a great goal. Be a Lemma—strive to be the best leader that you can be.

There is also Carissa, who is now a "regular" teenager but one who possesses the insight and personal strength of a matured leader. She doesn't yet fully recognize and appreciate the impact of the Life Lessons that she provides for others. Carissa is not yet at a point in her life where she focuses on teaching anyone else to lead, and it's not likely that she has formalized any plans for enhancing her leadership abilities. She just continues to live a "leading life" and to allow those around her to learn from her example. She just does it. Be a Carissa—live a leading life and allow others to see what leaders do by watching and learning from you.

This is the last chapter of the book, but certainly not the last chapter in your continuing quest to learn, grow, and lead well by listening to Life's Lessons. There will always be many people and situations that need your special gifts: yourself and your willingness and ability to provide the best in leadership.

Good leaders are the "fairest of them all." Look in the mirror. Who is the fairest of them all?

I think it's you.

Appendix

The recipes that I promised you. Enjoy!

The Best Blueberry Muffins

About 18 regular-sized muffins—eat some right away and freeze the rest!

Timing: Approximately 20 minutes plus 25 minutes for baking time

½ cup butter or margarine (doesnít matter) at room temperature
1 cup sugar
2 large eggs
1 tsp. vanilla
2 tsp. baking powder
½ tsp. salt
2 ½ cups blueberries—one, 12 oz. bag of frozen without the sugar added.
            Do not thaw.
2 cups all-purpose flour
½ cup milk

Topping: 1 T. sugar mixed with ¼ tsp. ground nutmeg

Grease muffin pans. Use lots of Pam—or the blueberries stick to the pan and are too hard to clean off. Beat butter with electric mixer until creamy. Add sugar and beat the mixture until pale and fluffy. Add eggs, one at a time, beating the mixture after each addition. Beat in vanilla, baking powder and salt. With a rubber spatula, fold half the flour, then half the milk into the batter. Repeat with the other half. Fold in the frozen blueberries.

Spoon batter into the cups, and sprinkle with the topping.
Bake at 375 degrees for 25–30 minutes or until muffins are golden brown and springy when you touch them.

Peach Cobbler

Ask your produce person for the right kind of peaches.

Timing: About 40 minutes plus 35 minutes for baking time. (But maybe youíd be faster. Kneading dough takes me too long!)

Peach Filling
8 cups pitted peaches, peeled and cut into sixths—approximately 12
        peaches
½ cup sugar
4 T. lemon juice
1 stick butter (½ cup)

Biscuit Topping
2 cups all-purpose flour
4 T. sugar
½ tsp. salt
4 tsp. baking powder
1 stick chilled butter (½ cup)
¾ cup milk (any kind of milk)

Preheat the oven to 425 degrees. Place the prepared peaches in a 9 x 13 baking pan and sprinkle them evenly with the sugar. Drizzle on the lemon juice and dot the peaches with the butter. Set aside while you make the biscuit topping.

Combine the flour, sugar, salt, and baking powder in a large mixing bowl and stir them together with a fork. Cut the butter into bits and drop it into the bowl. Using either a pastry blender, two knives (or your fingers, which is the easiest), work the butter into the flour mixture until the mixture resembles fine, even crumbs. (Donít worry about the tiny irregular bits and pieces.) Slowly add the milk, stirring constantly with a fork. Gather the dough together and place it on a lightly floured surface. Knead 8 to 10 times, until the dough is fairly smooth. Roll or pat the dough into a shape that will fit your dish. It should be no more than ½ in. thick, so trim the edges if necessary. Place the biscuit dough over the prepared fruit in the pan, pressing it down into the fruit all around the edges.

Bake at 425 degrees for 35–45 minutes, or until the juices are bubbling, the biscuit crust is golden brown, and the peaches are tender when pierced through the crust with a knife. Remove from the oven and place on rack. Serve warm if possible.

Serves 8 people or 6 of my family.

Sophia Loren's Pasta Carbonara

From her cookbook: *Sophia Loren's Recipes and Memories*

Timing: Fast! Starting boiling the water for the pasta as soon as you start sautéing the bacon!

1 T. olive oil
2 T. unsalted butter
8 oz. diced bacon

Heat the oil and butter in a pan, then add the bacon. Sauté over medium heat to brown the bacon well.

5–6 egg yolks (fresh eggs are recommended)
5 T. milk (whole or 2%)
3 T. grated Pecorino or Parmesan cheese

In a bowl, beat together the egg yolks, milk, and cheese.

1 pound of spaghetti

While the bacon is browning, cook the pasta al dente. Drain the pasta well, but do not rinse. Pour back into the pan, but not over the heat. Working quickly, first pour the bacon mixture from the sauté pan, then the beaten egg mixture over the pasta. Toss quickly to cover the strands of pasta with the sauce. The eggs will cook with the heat of the pasta. Serve immediately while still hot. Pass additional cheese at the table.

Serves 2, 3, or 4 depending on how hungry they are.

Beer Bread

Hearty bread—to-die-for toast and great with soup!

Timing: 5 minutes to assemble and mix, plus 45 minutes to bake. Add time to "warm" the beer.

12 oz. (one can) beer (any kind) at room temperature
3 cups self-rising flour
3 T. sugar

Stir together, mix well. Put into greased (Pam-sprayed) loaf pan.

Bake at 350 degrees for 45 minutes.

Homemade Chocolate Pudding

Pudding from a mix? Never again!

Timing: Approximately 10 minutes, and worth every minute!

6 T. sugar
3 T. cornstarch
3 cups milk (any kind of milk)
1 cup semisweet chocolate chips
1 T. vanilla extract

In a saucepan, combine sugar and cornstarch. Add milk and stir until smooth. Cook and stir over medium heat until mixture comes to a boil. Cook and stir 1–2 minutes longer or until thickened.

Stir in the chocolate chips. Cook and stir until melted. Remove from heat. Stir in vanilla. Spoon into dessert dishes or one beautiful serving bowl.

Serves: 4

Made in the USA